Spiritual Bypassing

When Spirituality Disconnects Us From what really matters

Robert Augustus Masters, PhD

EasyRead Large

Copyright Page from the Original Book

Copyright © 2010 by Robert Augustus Masters. All rights reserved. No portion of this book, except for brief review, may be reproduced, stored in a retrieval system, or transmitted in any form or by any means—electronic, mechanical, photocopying, recording, or otherwise—without the written permission of the publisher. For information contact North Atlantic Books.

PUBLISHED BY
North Atlantic Books
P.O. Box 12327
Berkeley, California 94712

Cover photo: redmal/istock.com
Cover and book design by Claudia Smelser
Printed in the United States of America

Spiritual Bypassing: When Spirituality Disconnects Us from What Really Matters is sponsored by the Society for the Study of Native Arts and Sciences, a nonprofit educational corporation whose goals are to develop an educational and cross-cultural perspective linking various scientific, social, and artistic fields; to nurture a holistic view of arts, sciences, humanities, and healing; and to publish and distribute literature on the relationship of mind, body, and nature.

North Atlantic Books' publications are available through most bookstores. For further information, visit our Web site at www.northatlanticbooks.com or call 800-733-3000.

LIBRARY OF CONGRESS CATALOGING-IN-PUBLICATION DATA

Masters, Robert Augustus.
  Spiritual bypassing : when spirituality disconnects us from what really matters / Robert Augustus Masters.
    p. cm.
  Includes index.
  ISBN 978-1-55643-905-6
  1. Avoidance (Psychology)—Religious aspects. 2. Psychotherapy—Religious aspects. 3. Spirituality—Psychology. I. Title.
  BL629.5.A76M37 2010
  204'.4—dc22
                                                            2010020598

1 2 3 4 5 6 7 8 9   Versa   15 14 13 12 11 10

TABLE OF CONTENTS

Additional praise for spiritual bypassing	i
ALSO BY ROBERT AUGUSTUS MASTERS	vi
AVOIDANCE IN HOLY DRAG	1
CUTTING THROUGH SPIRITUAL BYPASSING	14
LET'S STOP BEING NEGATIVE ABOUT OUR NEGATIVITY	24
BLIND COMPASSION	34
HEALTHY AND UNHEALTHY TRANSCENDENCE	46
CUTTING THROUGH SPIRITUAL SHORTCUTS	59
BRINGING SHADOW WORKOUT OF THE SHADOWS	69
WHAT GENERATES SPIRITUAL BYPASSING?	82
THE ANATOMY OF MAGICAL THINKING	91
WHY DON'T MORE SPIRITUAL TEACHERS INCLUDE PSYCHOTHERAPY IN THEIR WORK?	107
MAKING WISE USE OF ANGER	118
BOUNDARIES MAKE FREEDOM POSSIBLE	140
DON'T TAKE IT PERSONALLY?	156
RELEASING SEX FROM THE OBLIGATION TO MAKE US FEEL BETTER	164
NEITHER ROMANCING NOR FLEEING RELATIONSHIP	179
DISEMBODIED SPIRITUALITY AND EMBODIED BEING	190
TRUE RESPONSIBILITY	214
SPIRITUAL GULLIBILITY AND CULTISM	226
ARE WE RESPONSIBLE FOR OUR ILLNESS?	236
WHEN NONDUAL TEACHINGS ARE NOT NONDUAL	245
BRINGING SHAME OUT OF THE SHADOWS	255
WHEN OUR HONEYMOON WITH SPIRITUALITY IS OVER	271

THE METHOD OF NO METHOD	279
ILLUMINATING AND INTEGRATING BODY, MIND, EMOTION, AND SPIRITUALITY	291
ACKNOWLEDGMENTS	309
ABOUT THE AUTHOR	311
Back Cover Material	313
Index	317

Additional praise for spiritual bypassing

"In *Spiritual Bypassing*, Robert Augustus Masters offers a wakeup call—more of a shout—to those of us who have unwittingly fallen prey to all manner of promising and seductive antidotes to our pain and suffering in the form of detached spiritual teachings and New Age magical thinking. The book is a sobering and powerful reminder that our present embodiment, in all its flawed, messy humanness, cannot be conveniently sidestepped, and so invites us inward to a face-to-face encounter and embrace with the raw truth of who we really are. Masters' unique and at times disarming prose style blends a poetic sensibility with a surprising stark clarity that points us to 'What Really Matters.'"
—Eliezer Sobel, author of *The 99th Monkey: A Spiritual Journalist's Misadventures with Gurus, Messiahs, Sex, Psychedelics, and Other Consciousness-Raising Experiments*

"Traversing the muddy waters of contemporary spirituality requires a willingness to meet its seen and unseen challenges with ruthless self-honesty and keen discernment. Masters addresses 'the many faces of spiritual bypassing' with intellectual rigor, hard-earned insight, and emotional intelligence. It is a lucid, well-written, and practical guide for both new and seasoned practitioners on the spiritual path."
—Mariana Caplan, PhD, author of *Eyes Wide Open: Cultivating Discernment on the Spiritual Path* and *Halfway Up the Mountain: the Error of Premature Claims to Enlightenment*

"In *Spiritual Bypassing,* Robert Masters eloquently reminds us of something we have unknowingly misplaced on our spiritual journeys: Mother Earth. In our efforts to bypass our earthly challenges, we have disconnected from the Ground of our very being, seeking our wholeness on a pogo stick to the stars. In poignant and clarifying language, Masters calls us back home, confronting us with our

avoidance, inviting us to find our spirituality in the heart/depths of our humanness. In an era where detachment models for spirituality are becoming dangerously prevalent, his inclusive message is of profound importance. It may not appeal to the part of us that wants the path to be easy, but it will speak loudly to the part of us that longs for the truth. I recommend it wholeheartedly."
—Jeff Brown, author of *Soulshaping*

"Robert Masters has given us a great gift—a tremendously useful guide to examining our tendencies to spiritual bypassing, clearly the most comprehensive and accessible treatment available on this crucial topic. His work is a great contribution to the ongoing integration of psychotherapy and spiritual practice, and to our understanding of the meaning of spiritual maturity."
—Donald Rothberg, PhD, author of *The Engaged Spiritual Life*

"There is much hard-won wisdom in this work. *Spiritual Bypassing* is a

detailed, point-by-point description of how so-called spirituality can be used by some to actually avoid individuation, adulthood, and the *daimonic.* When Carl Jung noted that "neurosis is always a substitute for legitimate suffering," he hinted that, especially for the Western psyche, spiritual practice itself can be just such a sneaky neurosis. This insightful, firm, confrontive yet compassionate book promotes and encourages the complementary marriage of spiritual practice and psychotherapy, recognizing that they are—and, at best, have always been—basically two integrally related sides of the same existential coin: The most profound psychotherapy is essentially spiritual; and the deepest spiritual quest includes some depth psychology. Neither approach can be excluded on the unpredictable path toward selfhood."
—Stephen Diamond, PhD, author of *Anger, Madness, and the Daimonic: The Psychological Genesis of Violence, Evil, and Creativity*

"Uncompromising and truth-telling, this book is an antidote to spiritual

obesity. What emerges is the call to psychological clarity as essential to the mature spiritual life. Here is soul-fuel for those who would enter the road less traveled—the deeply examined life as part of spiritual practice."
—Jean Houston, PhD, author of *A Mythic Life*

ALSO BY ROBERT AUGUSTUS MASTERS

Darkness Shining Wild: An Odyssey to the Heart of Hell & Beyond Meditations on Sanity, Suffering, Spirituality & Liberation

Freedom Doesn't Mind Its Chains: Revisioning Sex, Body, Emotion & Spirituality

The Anatomy & Evolution of Anger: An Integral Exploration

Divine Dynamite: Entering Awakening's Heartland (revised edition)

Transformation Through Intimacy: The Journey Toward Mature Monogamy

Meeting The Dragon: Ending Our Suffering by Entering Our Pain

For all those whose longing to be truly free is becoming stronger than their desire to distract themselves from suffering

1

AVOIDANCE IN HOLY DRAG

An Introduction to Spiritual Bypassing

Spiritual bypassing, a term first coined by psychologist John Welwood in 1984, is the use of spiritual practices and beliefs to avoid dealing with our painful feelings, unresolved wounds, and developmental needs. It is much more common than we might think and, in fact, is so pervasive as to go largely unnoticed, except in its more obvious extremes.

Part of the reason for this is that we tend not to have very much tolerance, either personally or collectively, for facing, entering, and working through our pain, strongly preferring pain-numbing "solutions," regardless of how much suffering such "remedies" may catalyze. Because this preference has so deeply and thoroughly infiltrated our culture that it has become all but normalized, spiritual bypassing fits almost seamlessly into our collective habit of turning away from what is painful, as a kind of higher analgesic with seemingly minimal side effects. It is a spiritualized strategy not only for avoiding pain but also for legitimizing such avoidance, in ways ranging from the blatantly obvious to the extremely subtle.

Spiritual bypassing is a very persistent shadow of spirituality, manifesting in many forms, often without being acknowledged as such. Aspects of spiritual bypassing include exaggerated detachment, emotional numbing and repression, overemphasis on the positive, anger-phobia, blind or overly tolerant compassion, weak or too porous boundaries, lopsided development (cognitive intelligence often being far ahead of emotional and moral intelligence), debilitating judgment about one's negativity or shadow side, devaluation of the personal relative to the spiritual, and delusions of having arrived at a higher level of being.

The explosion of interest in spirituality since the mid-1960s, especially Eastern spirituality, has been accompanied by a corresponding interest and immersion in spiritual bypassing—which has, however, not very often been named, let alone viewed, as such. It has been easier to frame spiritual bypassing as a religion-transcending, spiritually advanced practice or perspective, especially in the fast-food spirituality epitomized by faddish phenomena like *The Secret.* Some of the more glaringly facile features, such as drive-through servings of reheated wisdom like "Don't take it personally" or "Whatever bothers you about someone is really only about you" or "It's all just an illusion," are available for consumption and parroting by just about anyone.

Happily, the honeymoon with false or superficial notions of spirituality is starting to wane. Enough bubbles have been burst; enough spiritual teachers, Eastern and Western, have been caught with pants or halo down; enough cults have come and gone; enough time has been spent with spiritual baubles, credentials, energy transmissions, and gurucentrism to sense deeper treasures. But valuable as the desire for a more authentic spirituality is, such change will not occur on any significant scale and really take root until spiritual bypassing is outgrown, and that is not as easy as it might sound, for it asks that we cease turning away from our pain, numbing ourselves, and expecting spirituality to make us feel better.

True spirituality is not a high, not a rush, not an altered state. It has been fine to romance it for a while, but our times call for something far more real, grounded, and responsible; something radically alive and naturally integral; something that shakes us to our very core until we stop treating spiritual deepening as something to dabble in here and there. Authentic spirituality is not some little flicker or buzz of knowingness, not a psychedelic blast-through or a mellow hanging-out on some exalted plane of consciousness, not a bubble of immunity, but a vast fire of liberation, an exquisitely fitting crucible and sanctuary, providing both heat and light for the healing and awakening we need.

Most of the time when we're immersed in spiritual bypassing, we like the light but not the heat. And when we're caught up in the grosser forms of spiritual bypassing, we'd usually much rather theorize about the frontiers of consciousness than actually go there, suppressing the fire rather than breathing it even more alive, espousing the ideal of unconditional love but not permitting love to show up in its more challenging, personal dimensions. To do so would be too hot, too scary, and too out-of-control, bringing things to the surface that we have long disowned or suppressed.

But if we really want the light, we cannot afford to flee the heat. As Victor Frankl said, "What gives light must endure burning." And being with the fire's heat doesn't just mean sitting with the difficult stuff in meditation, but also going into it, trekking to its core, facing and entering and getting intimate with whatever is there, however scary or traumatic or sad or raw.

We have had quite an affair with Eastern spiritual pathways, but now it is time to go deeper. We must do this not only to get more intimate with the essence of these wisdom traditions beyond ritual and belief and dogma but also to make room for the healthy evolution, not just the necessary Westernization, of these traditions so that their presentation ceases encouraging spiritual bypassing (however indirectly) and, in fact, consciously and actively ceases giving it soil to flower. These changes won't happen to any significant degree, however, unless we work in-depth and integratively with our physical, emotional, psychological, spiritual, and social dimensions to generate an ever-deeper sense of wholeness, vitality, and basic sanity.

Any spiritual path, Eastern or Western, that does not deal in real depth with psychological issues, and deal with these in more than just spiritual contexts, is setting itself up for an abundance of spiritual bypassing. If there is not sufficient encouragement and support from spiritual teachers and teachings for practitioners to engage in significant depth in psychoemotional work, and if those students who really need such work don't then do it, they'll be left trying to work out their psychoemotional issues, traumatic and otherwise, only through the spiritual practices they have been given, as if doing so is somehow superior to—or a "higher" activity than—engaging in quality psychotherapy. Psychotherapy is often viewed as an inferior undertaking relative to spiritual practice, perhaps even something we shouldn't have to do. When our spiritual bypassing is more subtle, the idea of psychotherapy may be considered more acceptable, but we will still shy away from a full-blooded investigation of our core wounds.

Spiritual bypassing is largely occupied, at least in its New Age forms, by the idea of wholeness and the innate unity of Being—"Oneness" being perhaps its favorite bumper sticker—but actually generates and reinforces fragmentation by separating out from and rejecting what is painful, distressed, and unhealed; all the far-from-flattering aspects of being human. By consistently keeping these in the dark, "down below" (when we're locked into our *head* quarters, our body and feelings seem to be below us), they tend to behave badly when let out, much like animals that have spent too long in cages. Our neglect of these aspects of ourselves, however gently framed, is akin to that of otherwise caring parents who leave their children without sufficient food, clothing, or care.

The trappings of spiritual bypassing can look good, particularly when they seem to promise freedom from life's fuss and fury, but this supposed serenity and detachment is often little more than metaphysical valium, especially for those who have made too much of a virtue out of being and looking positive.

A common telltale sign of spiritual bypassing is a lack of grounding and in-the-body experience that tends to keep us either spacily afloat in how we relate to the world or too rigidly tethered to a spiritual system that seemingly provides the solidity we lack. We also may fall into premature forgiveness and emotional dissociation, and confuse anger with aggression and ill will, which leaves us disempowered, riddled with weak boundaries. The overdone niceness that often characterizes spiritual bypassing strands it from emotional depth and authenticity; and its underlying grief—mostly unspoken, untouched, unacknowledged—keeps it marooned from the very caring that would unwrap and undo it, like a baby being readied for a bath by a loving parent.

Spiritual bypassing distances us not only from our pain and difficult personal issues but also from our own authentic spirituality, stranding us in a metaphysical limbo, a zone of exaggerated gentleness, niceness, and superficiality. Its frequently disconnected nature keeps it adrift, clinging to the life jacket of its self-conferred spiritual credentials. As such, it maroons us from embodying our full humanity.

But let us not be too hard on spiritual bypassing, for every one of us who has entered into the spiritual has engaged in spiritual bypassing, at least to some degree, having for years used other means to make ourselves feel better or more secure. Why would we not also approach spirituality, particularly at first, with much the same expectation that it make us feel better or more secure in various areas of our life?

To truly outgrow spiritual bypassing—which in part means releasing spirituality (and everything else!) from the obligation to make us feel better or more secure or more whole—we must not only see it for what it is and cease engaging in it but also view it with genuine compassion, however fiery that might be or need to be. The spiritual bypasser in us needs not censure nor shaming but rather to be consciously and caringly included in our awareness without being allowed to run the show. Becoming intimate with our own capacity for spiritual bypassing allows us to keep it in healthy perspective.

I have worked with many clients who described themselves as being on a spiritual path, particularly as meditators. Most were preoccupied, at least initially, with being nice, trying to be positive and nonjudgmental, while impaling themselves on various spiritual "shoulds," such as "I should not show anger" or "I should be more loving" or "I should be more open after all the time I've put into my spiritual practice." Fleeing their darker (or "less spiritual") emotions, impulses, and intentions, they had, to varying degrees, trapped themselves within the very practices and beliefs that they had hoped might liberate them, or at least make them feel better.

Even the most exquisitely designed spiritual methodologies can become traps, leading not to freedom but only to reinforcement, however subtle, of the "I" that wants to be a somebody who has attained or realized freedom (the very same "I" that doesn't realize there are no Oscars for awakening). The most obvious potential traps-in-waiting include the belief that we should rise above our difficulties and simply embrace Oneness, even as the tendency to divide everything into positive and negative, higher and lower, spiritual and nonspiritual, runs wild in us. Subtler traps-in-waiting, less densely populated with metaphysical lullabies and ascension metaphors, and cloaked in the appearance of discernment, teach non-aversion through cultivating a capacity for dispassionate witnessing and/or various devotional rituals. Subtler still are those that emphasize meeting everything with acceptance and compassion. Each approach has its own value, if only to eventually propel us into an even deeper direction, and each is far from immune to being possessed by spiritual bypassing, especially when we are still hoping, whatever our depth of spiritual practice, to reach a state of immunity to suffering (both personally and collectively).

As my spiritually inclined clients become more intimate with their pain and difficulties, coming to understand the origins of their troubles with a more open ear and heart, they either abandon their misguided spiritual practices and reenter a more fitting version of them with less submissiveness and more integrity and creativity or find new practices that better suit their needs, coming to recognize more deeply that everything—everything!—can serve their healing and awakening.

My purpose in writing this book is to present not just an anatomy of spiritual bypassing and its many faces but also to invite the outgrowing of it, so that we might enter a deeper life—a life of full-blooded integrity, depth, love, and sanity; a life of authenticity on every level; a life in which the personal, interpersonal, and transpersonal are all honored and lived to the fullest.

May what I have written serve you well.

CUTTING THROUGH SPIRITUAL BYPASSING

The first step in working with spiritual bypassing is to see it for what it is—employing spiritual beliefs to avoid dealing in any significant depth with our pain and developmental needs—and then to name it, so that we might begin relating *to* it rather than *from* it. This is relatively easy when spiritual bypassing manifests in its grosser forms, but not so easy when it gets more subtle, especially when it coexists with truly beneficial spiritual undertakings.

Uncovering and openly acknowledging our tendencies to spiritually bypass may trigger some shame in us at being "caught," but this is a healthy shame that we can readily work with as long as we don't allow it to fuel our inner critic. It helps to remember that spiritual bypassing isn't just something others do; it's something that we all have done. The freedom found in admitting its presence is akin to the freedom felt when we admit without any defensiveness that up until a moment ago we had been defensive in a heated exchange with a significant other.

Signs of spiritual bypassing at work are perhaps most commonly seen in the minimizing, superficializing, or outright negation of our shadow side and so-called negativity. Other behaviors include taking global or impersonal stands on clearly personal concerns, as when we might talk about the "fact" that everything is perfect, all unfolding exactly as it must, while we are talking to another in a demeaning way. Or in response to someone's suffering we may say, "It's all an illusion, including your suffering" or "It's just your ego," delivering one-liners with minimal feeling, much like newscasters reporting both the shallow and the deeply tragic in the very same professionally modulated tone of voice. By ducking into aphorisms of the absolute, we distance ourselves from their pain and our own.

Of course, not all spiritual bypassing is so emotionally disconnected, but the spiritually rationalized avoidance of feeling deeply, particularly with regard to our less pleasant emotions, is nonetheless a common indicator of it. Spiritual bypassing is especially common in spiritual paths that treat ego as something to eradicate, something in the way of spiritual realization, rather than an activity to illuminate and integrate with the rest of our being.

The greater the pain of our unresolved wounds, the greater the odds that we—if we are invested in being "spiritual" or in being viewed as "spiritual"—will manifest some kind of compensatory self-inflation (however humble its robes) and involve ourselves in spiritual bypassing in its grosser forms, wherein spiritual practice and attainment are used to avoid directly and unguardedly feeling the raw reality of suffering, keeping us dissociated or otherwise "safely" removed from our pain, especially the pain stemming from the more troubling times of our past. Many people get stranded here, assuming that if they are not feeling better from their spiritual practices, they have not gone deeply enough into them and must redouble their efforts. If this fails, their tendency is to blame themselves even as they resolutely cling to the demands and expectations of their spiritual path. Unpleasant though their spiritual shortfalls may be, such a focus keeps them distracted from having to face and deal with the bigger issue: their core pain.

More unfortunate than these practitioners are those who do "succeed" at spiritual bypassing—who not only consistently sidestep or otherwise avoid their core pain but also find a relatively steady comfort in their spiritual practices. I say "unfortunate" because given their degree of satisfaction, they are less likely than those who aren't succeeding at spiritual bypassing to take the plunge into working directly and deeply with their wounds and shadow elements.

When we're in the grip of spiritual bypassing, we tend to view psychotherapy as unnecessary, or only for the seriously neurotic, something that at best strengthens the very egoity that spirituality is supposed to cut through or eradicate. It is so easy to couch our fear of psychotherapy in spiritual language! Spiritual teachers who don't support their students in doing in-depth psychotherapy, perhaps because they themselves are ignorant about its process and benefits, are doing their students a huge disservice in overemphasizing the importance of doing spiritual practice, and spiritual practice only.

Spiritual bypassing keeps us stuck at a "higher" level that is really only higher in a conceptual sense. It's as if we are taking up residence on Floor 5 without having passed through Floors 2, 3, or 4. So we're occupying the fifth floor and have all the right furniture and accoutrements for that level, while the floors below us deteriorate due to our lack of attention and presence. Only when Floors 2, 3, and 4—unexplored and unoccupied—reach the point of undeniable, attention-grabbing disintegration do we start to realize our mistake and try to get back on track, however painful or humiliating that might be.

When transcendence of our personal history takes precedence over intimacy with our personal history, spiritual bypassing is inevitable. To not be intimate with our past—to not be deeply and thoroughly acquainted with our conditioning and its originating factors—keeps it undigested and unintegrated and therefore very much present, regardless of our apparent capacity for rising above it. Instead of trying to get beyond our personal history, we need to learn to relate to it with as much clarity and compassion as possible, so that it serves rather than obstructs our healing and awakening. This also means relating in similar fashion to our tendency to spiritually bypass, casting a lucid, caring eye upon the part of us who buys into it.

The tricky thing about spiritual bypassing is that it does not always look like spiritual bypassing. For example, if a spiritual teacher is asked by his students about difficulties they are having with integrating their spiritual practice and the demands of intimate relationship, and he provides them with only big-picture answers/truisms, waxing eloquently about the finite and the infinite, the nature of self, and so on, then he is engaged in spiritual bypassing, no matter how articulate and precise his answer may be, for he is, however inadvertently, avoiding dealing directly and relevantly with his students' personal and interpersonal pain, and probably his own as well.

Yes, his questioners may benefit somewhat from the overview he is presenting, but they are not getting anything suitably personal from him. The point here is not to avoid a big-picture answer but to provide one that is also a psychologically attuned, personally relevant answer. In spiritual bypassing's realm, conceptual spirituality more often than not masquerades as real spirituality. Conceptual or emotionally disconnected spirituality can be very comforting and safe, very easy to trot out, and very easy to use to rationalize our removal, especially emotionally, from the more difficult aspects of life.

Cutting through spiritual bypassing means turning toward the painful, disfigured, ostracized, unwanted, or otherwise disowned aspects of ourselves and cultivating as much intimacy as possible with them. To do this, we inevitably will have to deal with our numbness, approaching it with as much care as we can, ceasing to numb ourselves to our numbness. If doing so seems to break our heart, we are on the right path, even if we are on our hands and knees. For when our heart breaks, it doesn't shatter; it breaks open, expanding to include more and more. As we denumb, letting our heart remain raw, becoming more and more comfortable with our discomfort, we can see and feel what first drove us into spiritual bypassing. It would be an understatement to say that this is a challenging journey, for it asks of us a very deep vulnerability, a bareness of being to which we may not be at all accustomed.

Our unwillingness or inability to enter such vulnerability, to authentically connect with our childlike aspects (our innocence, wonder, prerational openness, et cetera), to feel genuine compassion for and connection with the child in us, especially when that child is hurt or traumatized, makes it very difficult, if not impossible, for us to truly touch and heartfully connect with the child in others. For that reason, we tend to keep our distance from those who are actively working with and through old childhood wounds, even when such work is clearly healing and potently integrative.

What spiritual bypassing would have us rise above is precisely what we need to enter, and enter deeply, with as little self-numbing as possible. To this end, it is crucial that we see through whatever practices we have, spiritual or otherwise, that tranquilize rather than illuminate and awaken us. Despite their undeniable calming and relaxing effects, meditative practices that sedate the mind can serve a detrimental purpose; feeling greater calm and relaxation is not necessarily always a good thing, particularly when it doesn't coexist with discernment and insight. Tranquilizers, meditative or otherwise, simply numb us, and if we have any investment in being numb, we may be drawn to meditative practices that keep us distant from our pain. As long as we are consciously and skillfully turning toward our pain and difficulties, staying close enough to them to work with them effectively, we will be less easily seduced by the desire to sedate ourselves.

Spiritual bypassing is more common than we might think; in fact, almost all of us who have engaged in spiritual disciplines have very likely done some time in spiritual bypassing's domain, especially when we were craving some distance from our everyday psychoemotional difficulties. Moving toward our pain may not feel good, but it is a necessary journey if we are to truly heal, through which our wounds and difficulties serve rather than hinder us.

Spiritual bypassing is not something to eradicate, but it is something to outgrow. Let us treat it as such, recognizing that real spirituality is not an escape but rather an arrival.

LET'S STOP BEING NEGATIVE ABOUT OUR NEGATIVITY

There isn't any such thing as a negative emotion.

There are negative things that we *do* with our emotions, but our emotions themselves are neither negative nor positive. They simply are.

Consider anger. When we are hostile, we emit unmistakable negativity, bristly and mean-spirited, tight and heartless—but to take this as an example of anger being a negative emotion misses the mark. Yes, we are angry, but we are filtering—and forcing—it through a darkly twisted lens, so that it is expressed not as clean anger (that is, anger free of aggression, blaming, and shaming) but as hostility. That is, we are doing something with our anger, something that holds and channels it in a negative context.

Does this mean that anger itself is therefore a negative emotion? No. It means we have handled our anger negatively, putting a mean-spirited spin on it. Our choice. Hostility is not a negative emotion but rather a negative framing and expression of an emotion, namely anger.

Anger itself can be a positive force: Getting angry that you have just lost your job may give you the energy and sheer drive to pursue more fitting work, which is obviously a positive thing. Likewise, getting angry about the abuse you are suffering in a relationship will help fuel you to form healthy boundaries, providing much of the motivation and strength needed to either improve the relationship or leave it.

Take hatred. There's no doubt as to its negativity. But is it an emotion? Or is it something that we are *doing* with emotion? Hatred is not just anger or hurt or a mix of the two, but rather a combination of anger and hurt darkly contracted in a situation where an offending person (or people) has become the object of our hatred. So hatred is something that we *do* with emotion; we are not just saying that we are angry and that we are hurt, but are conveying this in a very negative and sometimes violent manner. There is a lot of energy in hate; it can be very passionate. And it also can be very consuming (especially in its uglier or more obsessive forms), eating away at us, taking us so far down that it becomes our state of being, not just an occasional reaction to difficult circumstances.

None of this is to say, however, that hatred is something we should always try to get over as quickly as possible. Sometimes we need to openly feel and express our hatred (under suitable conditions) in order to heal and move on; for example, if someone has just murdered our child, it is natural, at least for a while, to hate that person; natural to be fueled with a great intensity of rage and grief, natural to want to hurt or even kill the murderer. If we allow ourselves to express these feelings in an appropriate setting, such as with a skilled psychotherapist, we will, sooner or later, not just break down but break open until we are grief incarnate, making room for our woundedness without being overrun or governed by it.

This of course takes time, but not nearly as much time as when we let our hatred out partially or only in ways that reinforce it, so that it festers and feeds upon itself, encoding its will throughout us. Those who fully express their hatred in a sane manner, without doing harm to themselves or others, are far more capable of real forgiveness than those who keep their hatred locked in or try to rise above it prematurely, leaving a considerable woundedness unhealed beneath their forced equanimity.

So the road to genuine forgiveness is often paved with hatred. But go to the heart of hate and you won't find hate but rather great heart-wrenching grief, a broken-open depth of being that is both agonizingly and exquisitely painful, soberingly spacious, and eventually liberating. It is through this fire that forgiveness becomes not just some paint-by-numbers spiritual bypassing activity but a tremendously powerful and empowering practice. Those of us caught up in spiritual bypassing tend to slap the labels of "positive" and "negative" onto emotions as if such qualities were absolute givens. But the more we investigate the reality of our lives, the clearer it becomes that ascribing qualities like "negative" and "positive" to emotions is inevitably a context-bound undertaking.

And yet the lure of idealized spirituality remains strong, leading us to seek expansion in almost all things in the belief that expansion is positive, contraction negative; that expansion lifts us and contraction sinks us; that expansion epitomizes *yes,* contraction *no;* that expansion is "higher," contraction "lower;" that expansion frees us while contraction entraps us; and so on.

But there is nothing inherently virtuous about expansion—think of imperialism and colonization, as well as of metastasizing cancer cells—nor anything inherently unvirtuous about contraction. Expansion and contraction are more intertwined than we might think; when we inhale, for example, it may seem as if all that is happening is an expansion of our torso to draw in more air, but there is also a contraction of our nasal tissues and upper throat, which tighten up a bit as we inhale. Every movement we make includes both. In spiritual bypassing's realm, however, expansion is still held as something better than contraction, as exemplified by our enthusiasm for "expanded" consciousness.

Perhaps our most contracted emotion is fear (with shame a not-so-distant second). We tend to view fear as negative, resisting its downward pull, numbing ourselves as much as possible to the presence and raw feeling of fearfulness. In many ways, spiritual bypassing is just another strategy to avoid fear, using the anesthetizing capacity of emotional disconnection as its primary tool. But if we stay present with fear's energies and intentions, letting ourselves openly feel and track its sensations and coursings through our body rather than falling into its grip, we will become less fearful of our fear.

Many of us are afraid we'll get stuck or lost in fear if we move closer to it, but what actually happens when we consciously enter our fear, step by step, is that it ceases to grip us so tightly. The more deeply we move into our fearfulness, wearing our attentiveness like a miner's headlamp, the less fearful we become. When we remain outside or removed from our fear, we are trapped by it, but when we actually do get inside, cultivating intimacy with it, we are no longer entrapped by it, discovering—and not just intellectually—that it is but darkly contracted energy, a knotted-up vitality that can be freed when we become intimate with it.

Being negative about our negativity fragments us, stranding us from our unresolved wounds. Hurt, rage, grief, shame, fear, terror, loneliness, despair, and so on—all of these tend to get lumped together as "negativity," as something far from spiritual. It's as if we have abandoned the child in us, fleeing that little one's pain, helplessness, and longing for safety and love in the name of a supposedly more mature or spiritual approach. But all we've really done is escape from the very pain that, if fully felt and skillfully approached, would free us to live more deeply and more fully and, yes, more spiritually. Our lack of intimacy with our anger, fear, shame, doubt, terror, loneliness, grief, and other painful states keeps our experience superficial, emotionally anemic, and addicted to whatever helps numb us to our negativity.

Such a flight from our more painful emotions is, of course, not limited to spiritual bypassing but characterizes much of our culture (especially in the form of addiction). Some of us may flip to the other extreme and act out our painful emotions, expressing them irresponsibly, thereby giving a bad name to such feelings when in reality the real problem lies with our indulgence in their unskillful expression. Those enmeshed in spiritual bypassing will often use such examples of overreaction to justify their own emotional disconnection and dissociation.

The real concern isn't whether or not to express our "negative" feelings but how we choose to express them. Repressed anger is implicated in various illnesses (weakening the immune system), but so too is over-expressed anger (think hostility). Beyond the polarities of holding our anger in and directly expressing our anger is the possibility of a truly healthy capacity for both containment and release of anger that is infused with compassion, clarity, and vitality.

So turn toward your negativity. Stop pathologizing it, stop relegating it to a lower status, stop keeping it in the dark. Go to it, open its doors and windows, take it by the hand. Meet its gaze. Feel its woundedness, feel into it, feel for it, feel it without any buffers. Soon you will start to sense that its gaze is none other than your own, perhaps from an earlier time, but yours nonetheless, containing so much of you. Humanize it fully. Keep something in the dark long enough and it will probably behave badly.

Turn on the lights, slowly but surely. Your simple presence is enough. Let your heart soften. Breathe a little more deeply, bringing what you call your negativity closer to you, opening at a fitting pace. No rush. Let it shift, however slowly, from a distant foreign object to a reclaimed part of your being. Let its pain and longing break your heart. Your ambition to transcend your negativity is now all but gone, as you realize right to your core that your true work is to reclaim and reembody it. You are with yourself more deeply, your initial aversion all but gone, and now hold what you previously termed your negativity in the way that loving parents hold their distressed child, bringing it into your heart, feeling a rising desire and power to protect that little one. No negativity now. Just love, ease, recognition, presence, effortless wholeness. This is life in the raw, too real to be reduced to positive and negative, too alive to be shut down.

BLIND COMPASSION

Neurotic Tolerance in Caring's Robes

Given how essential compassion is to the well-being of one and all, we need to access and practice it as much as possible. To do so requires that we know compassion well, being familiar (and more than just intellectually so) not only with what constitutes it but also with what constitutes its imitators, among which are pity (a condescending, fear-infused, let's-keep-the-suffering-others-at-a-distance concern) and blind compassion (an exaggeratedly tolerant, confrontation-phobic, undiscriminating attempt at caring). While not everyone who is enmeshed in spiritual bypassing is a practitioner of blind compassion, the spiritualized avoidance of pain and anger, however conscious or unconscious, does habitually run rampant in our culture.

Blind compassion is rooted in the belief that we are all doing the best that we can. When we are driven by blind compassion, we cut everyone far too much slack, making excuses for others' behavior and making nice in situations that require a forceful "no," an unmistakable voicing of displeasure, or a firm setting and maintaining of boundaries. These things can, and often should, be done out of love, but blind compassion keeps love too meek, sentenced to wearing a kind face. This is not the kindness of the Dalai Lama, which is rooted in courage, but rather a kindness rooted in fear, and not just the fear of confrontation, but also the fear of not coming across as a good or spiritual person.

When we are engaged in blind compassion we rarely show any anger, for we not only believe that compassion has to be gentle, we are also frightened of upsetting anyone, especially to the point of their confronting us. This is reinforced by our judgment of anger, especially in its more fiery forms, as something less than spiritual; something to be equated with ill will, hostility, and aggression; something that should not be there if we were being truly loving. Blind compassion reduces us to harmony junkies, entrapping us in unrelentingly positive expression.

With blind compassion we don't know how to—or won't learn how to—say "no" with any real power, avoiding confrontation at all costs and, as a result, enabling unhealthy patterns to continue. Our "yes" is then anemic and impotent, devoid of the impact it could have if we were also able to access a clear, strong "no" that emanated from our core. When we mute our essential voice, our openness is reduced to a permissive gap, an undiscerning embrace, a poorly boundaried receptivity, all of which indicate a lack of compassion for ourselves (in that we don't adequately protect ourselves). Blind compassion confuses anger with aggression, forcefulness with violence, judgment with condemnation, caring with exaggerated tolerance, and moral maturity with spiritual correctness.

By reducing the ultimate truth of our real nature to mere concepts and then undiscerningly applying these to the neurotic or abusive behavior of others, spiritually whitewashing or otherwise downplaying such behavior while eviscerating our response to it (an alarmingly naive yet not uncommon example being: "You should not be angry at your rapist because he is really just part of you and you are just part of him—we're all one."), we remain morally deluded and disempowered, incapable of needed confrontation. But in doing so, we find a safety from the more brutal dimensions of life that we crave.

Much of this behavior has to do with the popularized notion that we shouldn't judge others. There are some very serious problems with this kind of thinking: First of all, we *do* judge others; judgment is simply one of the things that the mind does. So to make it wrong—that is, to judge our judging—only drags us into guilt's domain, splitting us into "good" (read: not judging) and "bad" (read: judging) factions. The mind—your mind, my mind, everyone's mind—will keep churning out judgments because that's its nature. What really matters is how we handle our judgments: Do we identify with them? Do we take them seriously, and if so, when? Do we allow them to recruit emotional energy? Do we try to rise above them, or pretend that they aren't there? In short, judging others is not the real issue; what is truly important is how we deal with our judgments. Since they are already there, why not make wise or life-giving use out of them instead of trying to get rid of them?

The second problem with the notion that we shouldn't judge others is the fact that judgment per se is not necessarily a negative phenomenon. Strip away the hostile, condescending, or mean-spirited elements that often characterize judgment and you may find a kernel of valuable insight, or perhaps a timely intuition, amidst what is left. Judgment is not necessarily equivalent to condemnation!

If we see others behaving abusively or know for certain that they have done so and judgment arises in us, we'd do well not to beat ourselves up, for that reaction is a natural part of our moral response. If we look closely, we will see that we are not so much judging them as we are judging their behavior—but in any case, we are judging. And this is a major no-no for those of us who are stuck in blind compassion, even as we scramble to distance or dissociate ourselves from our own judging. If someone has just assaulted our child, are we going to make a problem out of the fact that we are judging that person and that we are outraged? Are we going to bypass our feelings for what has happened by framing the whole thing in a "higher" light before we have even dealt with the raw reality of it? Probably not, unless we are committed to blind compassion.

When those who engage in blind compassion encounter or hear about offensive behavior in others, they usually take pains not only to be nonjudgmental—or at least not to say or do anything that could be construed as judgmental—but also to examine how their reaction might reflect their own shortcomings. That is, if what you are doing is upsetting me, my job is not to focus on your behavior but only to investigate what my being bothered says about me, perhaps even appreciating the opportunity you are giving me to examine myself.

This is not only a misguided reading of the art of allowing all things to serve our awakening, but a far-from-compassionate response to those who have offended us. For in not doing what we can to bring people face to face with the consequences of their actions, we are actually depriving them of something that they may sorely need. Furthermore, in letting them off the hook, we are doing the same for ourselves.

Those of us who practice blind compassion generally spiritualize our misguided tolerance and aversion to confrontation, confusing being loving with putting up with whatever anyone does and never judging them, no matter what. Even clearly abusive behavior on the part of a spiritual teacher may be excused as an opportunity for students to grow in their practice. We are so afraid of our darker aspects that we keep trying to paint them over with our best qualities, not realizing that our narrow ideas of proper "spiritual" expression limit our ability to respond appropriately and robustly to life.

Some who act from blind compassion may do so for reasons of survival, having learned as children that the best way to deal with confrontational or violent situations was to make nice and to make excuses for the abusive behavior of others (perhaps having learned this by example from a parent who was passively receiving abuse from the other parent). Such people will often say of their parents that they were doing the best that they could—even when this "best" included extremes of abuse—frequently citing their parents' own less-than-ideal upbringing. Believing in this allows us to leave our parents' mistreatment of us unchallenged (which makes the child in us feel safer but still not truly safe). We may say that we don't want to hurt them, that we see no point in bringing up the past with them, that what they did was just a product of their past, and so on, excuse upon excuse.

To cut through this, at some point we would have to not only openly feel the pain of what we suffered but also feel its consequences later in our life, and not many of us want to do that, even when we understand the value of doing so. We learned back then that saying a clear "no" to the hurt that we were suffering often only made things even worse. So as adults we continue to avoid saying "no," fearing, however unconsciously, that doing so is very dangerous (because for many of us it truly was dangerous when we were children). Practicing blind compassion keeps us "safely" removed both from having to say a strong and unequivocal "no" and from the consequences of doing so.

The belief that everyone is doing the best they can lets everyone off the hook, including us—this way, we don't have to ruffle any feathers, raise any hackles, kick up a storm, make a fuss, or otherwise confront anybody. Such a belief robs us of autonomy and accountability, implying as it does that we don't really have a choice in what we do. If we view our parents as puppets of their conditioning, how can we hold them responsible for what they did? After all, they couldn't help it—or could they? There is also a fear of recognizing that our parents did make a choice when they hurt us, for if we see this, what are we going to do? Can we then remain passive children in adult bodies (*adulterated,* so to speak, by our unresolved wounds)?

Blind compassion frames us as victims and enables us to stay that way even as it delivers spiritual platitudes about our true nature and our inherent goodness. Blind compassion disempowers us while giving power to the offending other, whereas real compassion empowers us to take the necessary action, however painful that might be. Real compassion can be fierce when it needs to be, without any loss of heart. For example, if I am being extremely reactive with you, trashing our relationship with abandon, you might meet me with a force of equivalent intensity, stopping me in my tracks with a "Stop!" that is as fiery as it is caring. You might not appear caring as you say this, but I can feel it as you interrupt my neurotic ritual. And it doesn't take long for me to appreciate the fact that you care enough to have confronted me with such fierce compassion.

Those of us engaging in blind compassion mean well. Unfortunately, our efforts to do good only backfire. In our hurry to forgive we skip the process that leads to authentic forgiveness—feeling our hurt, expressing our needs, and perhaps navigating conflict. When we don't make sufficient room for the unfolding and expression of what must precede forgiveness, we tend to confuse forgiveness with condoning, trying in the name of acceptance to pardon those who have hurt us before their behavior has been examined and felt in any real depth.

Blind compassion takes many forms and can be found in every area of life, worsening the very conditions it supposedly seeks to alleviate. So get familiar with blind compassion. See it, name it, and don't blame it. After that, meet it and its underlying fear with genuine compassion—compassion that's willing to be fiery, fierce, unsmiling if need be, and loving enough to not limit itself to being nice.

As we shed our blinders and clearly see our pain—our anger and hurt and frustration and moral outrage—we reenter a realm of love that had been closed off but from which we can now freely give and receive. We express a genuine compassion with spine and heart, and with an especially keen and caring eye for those who are still under the spell of blind compassion.

HEALTHY AND UNHEALTHY TRANSCENDENCE

To transcend something is to go beyond it to the point of ceasing to identify with it, so that it becomes an object of our awareness. When this process is healthy, what's been transcended is not excluded from our being (any more than clouds are excluded from the sky) but rather is "repositioned" and related to in ways that serve our well-being. When transcendence is unhealthy, what has been transcended is excluded from our being, resulting in escapism and disconnection. Where healthy transcendence embraces what's been transcended, unhealthy transcendence avoids it, making a spiritual virtue out of rising above whatever is deemed "lower" or "darker" elements of our nature. This is dissociation disguised in holy drag.

For those of us caught in spiritual bypassing, transcendence is an unquestioned virtue; however premature or unhealthy it might be, this spiritual ideal is maintained by a steady diet of ascension metaphors. It is easy to get seriously psyched about rising above whatever is difficult or painful for us, granting exaggerated importance to the notion of ascension and its imperative of "up-ness"—making spiritual points out of charged moments of up-ness, keeping our head so up that our body appears to be way "down there." This ungrounded orientation to life pulls us "higher" without anchoring us to anything substantial. If we are feeling something like heartbreak that "brings us down," instead of letting ourselves really feel and openly express this, we instead rise up, floating above our hurt, disconnecting from it to the point of barely feeling it, while conceiving of our flight as a spiritual and legitimate going-beyond.

Not surprisingly, the opposite of ascension—which we might call descension—is not very popular with those engaged in spiritual bypassing.

Descending into our darker elements may be construed as a "downer" or a slippage, a failure, a dropping into the "lower." We tend to either pathologize down-ness (especially when it shows up as negativity, fear, depression, shame, or contraction) or keep it at a considerable distance, as if it is just some sort of noxious or unwholesome substance. To those of us enmeshed in spiritual bypassing, "up" almost always represents expansion and freedom and positivity—the "higher"—and "down" is contraction and entrapment and negativity—the "lower."

Viewing being down (as when we are depressed or in turmoil) as something negative, something far from spiritual, turns being up (as when we are on a roll or are immersed in being positive) into an exaggeratedly important quality, to be held aloft even when circumstances clearly call for something very different (as when anger is clearly needed)—such is one of the key binds in which spiritual bypassing deposits us.

Getting more intimate with our "lower" qualities—all those things that we may think we should be transcending—is not a particularly popular topic for those of us enamored of spiritual bypassing. In fact, it's such a downer that it's usually only handled with spiritual tongs, lifted and dropped into sterilized vats brimming with affirmations, meditational tranquility, and other uplifting strategies, as if there's nothing to be done with the "lower" other than converting it to something "higher" (much like indigenous tribes in the hands of European missionaries).

But for all our reverence for what we conceive of as being higher, we can very easily spend an abundance of time looking down (although we might argue that when we are so loftily situated, most of what we are looking at is inevitably lower down), and not just geographically. Unfortunately, we do not actually descend or go down to any significant degree, but rather just look—or cast our "I"—in that direction, gazing down with intellectual compassion (and perhaps more than a trace of spiritual elitism) at all the wayward souls and unspiritual activities below.

There is no way that we, given our involvement in spiritual bypassing, are actually going to leave its tower, its headquarters, its bastion of immunity, its insulated certainties. There's just too much pain down below. Who wants to openly feel that?

In spiritual bypassing, descending to any noticeable degree into what is troubling or eating at us is usually held to be all but synonymous with failing or sinking, being merely a sign of regression—unless of course we lower ourselves just enough to help uplift those who are already down below (which is not much more than a Pollyannaish slumming of the "higher" leaving a few Christmas loaves for the "lower").

But having to stay "up" cuts us off from our roots, our history, our ground. Having to stay "up" dilutes and impoverishes us, leaving us to feed mostly on recycled spiritual clichés and other heady souvenirs of secondhand living. Up, up, and away we float to avoid our pain and developmental challenges, stuffing ourselves with spiritual knowledge—confusing information with transformation—while our body pays the price of being only superficially lived at best. Thus we forget that "down" is not "up" having a bad day, but rather where seeds flourish and roots grow deep.

"Down" is much more than the trash bin for what we cannot stand about ourselves, much more than the hangout for what we have disowned in ourselves, and much more than the darkened place where we keep what we have ostracized, condemned, or otherwise rejected in ourselves. "Down" is where so much of our genuine growth takes root, waiting for our participatory recognition of its value. Through aligning ourselves with such re-cognition, meeting and embracing what we have turned away from in ourselves, we make room for real transformation.

The upside of "down" is the extraordinarily fertile opportunity that it provides. For many of us on a spiritual path, our body tends to be "down there," relegated to the status of an "it." Whether we take care of it or not, we tend not to live in a truly embodied way (that is, in intimate, well-grounded contact with our physicality and emotions) unless we've freed ourselves from spiritual bypassing's grip. We may even conceive of our body as just a container for our soul or spirit, forgetting that what we actually are is not in a body but rather is making an appearance *as* a body.

Getting more embodied, and not just physically, means making deeper and deeper contact with what we are feeling, and this is sometimes far from pleasant. It's easier to float near it, to dissociate from it, and to make such distancing—such emotional disconnection—into a spiritual virtue. But fleeing or marginalizing our more painful emotional states is of no more use than is exploiting the feel-good possibilities of our embodiment (as when we lose ourselves in eroticism).

Those who have embraced spiritual bypassing fail to realize that healthy transcendence is neither a flight nor a severing or disconnection from "lower" things and qualities but rather a going beyond them that does not exclude them. With this radical inclusion, we expand both horizontally and vertically, expanding ourselves to include a particular quality while at the same time not identifying with it. There is separation in this, and there is also connection; in fact, both co-arise, both coexist, both function in mutual resonance. For example, if we are reactively angry, right at the edge of hostility, we can step back from it just state, almost as if engaging in dialogue with that angry aspect of ourself. We do not exclude that angry "I" but are sufficiently expansive now to include it without letting it overcome us. We are both apart from that angry "I" and connected to it. We have not fled it, but have rooted ourselves in a perspective that allows us to see our anger clearly and to work with it more cleanly.

Those who ardently believe in Oneness and nonseparation tend to divide rather than unify, separate rather than integrate, detaching themselves from whatever they deem to be lower or less evolved or negative. Trying to get away from such qualities, thereby refusing to develop any sort of in-depth relationship with them, keeps us fragmented, stranded from embodying genuine wholeness. Such is the price we pay when we let ourselves be taken over by spiritual bypassing.

The detachment that characterizes healthy transcendence is not at all dissociative, keeping us close enough to whatever is being transcended to know it well and just far enough away to be able to see it clearly, to bring it into lucid focus. By contrast, spiritual bypassing keeps us so removed that we are unable to cultivate any significant intimacy with our experience. For various reasons (likely rooted in our early years), we may have a preference for such distancing, but sooner or later, the need or ability to maintain that distance usually lessens, and we come into closer proximity with what we have avoided.

Transcending something in ourselves does not necessarily mean that it no longer arises in or occupies us. Instead it is energetically repositioned in our being and we relate to it rather than identify with it. What was subject is now object; before, we were acting and speaking as if we were it, and now we are aware *of* it. That is, we have gone beyond it without losing touch with or excluding it from ourselves. By bringing some caring into this process, some love, we achieve intimacy with that quality in us. Thus, we do not simply detach from an emotion like fear but remain lucidly engaged with it. Holding our fear (and our fearful self) with both spaciousness and compassion serves us well.

Spiritual bypassing's version of transcendence turns whatever has been transcended into a disowned object—an "it." Healthy transcendence, on the other hand, turns whatever has been transcended into another aspect of our true self, not disowning it but recognizing it as reclaimed "I." Choosing this path of transcendence results in a rare intimacy, in which our embrace of our intrinsic Unity of Being does not separate or alienate us from our differences but holds them in healthy perspective.

In spiritual bypassing we cling to "higher" beliefs—forgetting that even the most sublime belief is still just a belief—but real transcendence goes beyond belief by exposing, illuminating, and unhousing that in us which is doing the believing, which we might call the "believer" (not really an entity but an activity, an undertaking). This exposure and decentralizing of the believer means that it can no longer masquerade as us. We do not get rid of it but rather relocate it so that it no longer runs the show. We do not look down upon the believer in us but instead choose to cultivate intimacy with it, recognizing it as an idiosyncratic, vital aspect of who we are.

What happens to our beliefs when the believer in us is seen for what it is? They may still arise, but their hold on us is far less tight, giving us more room to breathe. There is life beyond belief, and it doesn't require that we have no beliefs but that we see them for what they are and respond to them accordingly. Seeing our beliefs and their animating forces for what they are is essential for cutting through spiritual bypassing, if only because spiritual bypassing is so rigidly and unquestioningly centered on its beliefs.

The very "I"—or apparent self—behind our spiritual bypassing tendencies must itself be exposed and transcended if we are to spiritually awaken. When we do this, we open ourselves to the pain, the sense of lack, and the raw hurt that originally animated that "I," that broken aspect of self. Through this opening, we enter the heart of our core wounding until it no longer so compellingly generates "solutions" (like over-intellectualization, spiritual bypassing, workaholism, substance abuse, eroticism, and so on) to itself.

In the genesis of such transcendence, our pathway is not necessarily straightforward—we don't just ascend, we also descend, moving from ascending to descending to here-ing (moving from here to here, from now to now), excluding nothing from our being without letting any of it get in the driver's seat. There is no turning away, not even from our turning away. Difficult qualities are divested of their viewpoint without robbing them of their essential energy, so that they shift from unwanted things or "its" to reclaimed us. Healthy transcendence makes ample room for this process while at the same time keeping a consistently clear and compassionate eye on it.

As we have seen, "Up, up, and away" is the mantra for unhealthy transcendence. What is the mantra for healthy transcendence? "Going beyond all, excluding none." The heart has more than enough room for it all.

CUTTING THROUGH SPIRITUAL SHORTCUTS

Spiritual bypassing frequently presents itself as an opportunity to fast-track spiritual progress, a shortcut through delusion to enlightenment. The real delusion here, of course, is the very idea that one can actually cut corners in spiritual practice. All of our attempts to dodge the messy world of difficult relationships, unpleasant emotions, and whatever else we would rather avoid only sidetrack and obstruct us, eventually generating enough suffering to draw us back to the steps we skipped or only partially took—of honoring, digesting, embodying, and integrating the essential lessons in our lives.

Not surprisingly, those of us enmeshed in spiritual bypassing do not view ourselves as cutting corners but rather as cutting through whatever is extraneous, not wasting time in activities that drag us down or pull us into the past. The trouble with this view is that many of the activities we consider irrelevant are in fact necessary for our evolution. For example, we may have a pattern of picking emotionally unavailable partners, a pattern with which we keep energetically aligning ourselves, even when we know better. We would rather not get intimate with and work through this pattern (especially in psychotherapeutic contexts), instead employing various means to disengage from it, including such "remedies" as repeating affirmations (like "I am attracting my perfect partner"), doing meditative practices that tranquilize us, simply letting the issue drift to the periphery of our priorities, or focusing on unconditional love and idealized intimacy instead (which leaves our pull to emotionally unavailable partners festering on the outskirts of our hope)—whatever helps keep us from the pain of relational dysfunction and the pain of failed intimacy.

If we are in the grip of spiritual bypassing, our rationalizations for why we don't have a partner or why we remain in a deeply troubled, stagnant relationship usually go unchallenged—no rocking of the boat, no shaking of the tree, no shift from being nice to being authentic, no descent into our hurt, no breakthrough into real integrity. To work through our attraction to emotionally unavailable partners, we need to turn toward that pattern and get to its roots—exposing and unguardedly feeling both its origins and the pain that first animated it. This journey, if engaged with depth and clarity rather than just as an intellectual exercise, does not leave us stranded in our past but liberates us from mechanically choosing yet another emotionally unavailable partner.

This is not just a psychological undertaking but also a spiritual one, which awakens us to our conditioning and its underlying mechanics with clarity. With this understanding we can take charge of our charge regarding the kind of partner we really want, so that the intensity of our pull toward another does not automatically determine our actions as it once did.

Trying to compensate for our lack of relational intimacy by vaulting ourselves into various ideals of relationship, romanticizing the notion of perfect partners, tantric bliss, and unconditional love, and claiming that this "leap" really has deposited us at a higher level is akin to saying that we have reached the top of Mount Everest when in fact we've just been comfortably helicoptered there for a brief, well-insulated landing. Not having taken the climb, and thus not having engaged in any of the lessons of such a challenging trek, leaves us far less capable of appreciating where we are than if we had actually made the climb. Our helicoptered self has found a shortcut, but in doing so has lost out on the grounding and embodiment and participatory knowingness that can be gained only through the climb itself. (This can also be said about those who repeatedly use psychedelics to reach a peak experience.) Theoretically we may have arrived, but with so little of ourselves actually there, we cannot call it a true arrival.

There may be an abundance of Everests in spiritual bypassing's trophy case, but they are as lifeless as the glassy-eyed heads decorating the walls of big-game hunters—nice to look at and to reminisce about, but little more.

Smaller peaks are not usually very interesting to those of us caught up in spiritual bypassing; the idea of big steps, big leaps, big changes is much more tantalizing. Working in-depth with the differences between anger and aggression, tracing the origins and evolution of a reactive tendency, or getting genuinely vulnerable, hold far less allure than the pursuit of spiritual powers and enlightenment.

Where some of us get stuck by becoming overly preoccupied with psychological issues and unhappy feelings, spiritual bypassers often get stuck in Big Picture and Grand Scheme fixations, keeping their gaze fixed upward so they don't have to see or give attention to those nasty pulls from below.

Those who have turned spiritual bypassing into a business—profiting, for example, from people's belief in positive thinking—are usually far from shy about advertising it, which they refer to not as spiritual bypassing but as spiritual opportunity. They sell it as a shortcut and a great deal, the packaging of which is saturated with Big Picture promises, hyperenthused testimonials, and related marketing hype, most of which is all about us, the hungry spiritual consumers, getting in on a fantastic, specially-priced-just-for-us deal that guarantees, with not all that much effort, a stupendous life, a life of ease, abundance, love, and spiritual awakening. Wow! And the sooner the better—why miss out on the early-bird discount?

Spiritual bypassing's entrepreneurs and gurus did not, however, arrive at such marketing success without some serious inspiration from—and abundant overlapping with—the self-help industry, which pioneered the packaging of personal-growth shortcuts. Although spiritual bypassers might look down on the crasser, more embarrassingly materialistic elements of the self-help industry, spiritual bypassing is arguably the very same industry decked out in more spiritually fashionable garb, mouthing many of the same platitudes about making a difference, or being of service, or giving back, with enough of a metaphysical overlay to give all the hype a greater patina of respectability.

As much as spiritual bypassing is presented as a shortcut, it is just a detour, a wandering away from what truly matters, a hanging out in metaphysical cul-de-sacs, providing not much more than empty calories and a seat in the uppermost bleachers, exploiting the fast-food, get-it-now mentality that pervades contemporary culture. As such, its devotees offer a spiritual fillup, a real deal at the pumps, a respite from the collective sense of overwhelm and not-so-distant dread that, however subtly, eats away at us.

We are in such a hurry to get it, whatever *it* may be. Greed for speed—fast food, fast money, fast relationships, fast spirituality. Drive-through divinity with organic fries and easy-to-swallow highs. Who wants to spend years doing spiritual practices when the same results can apparently be gained—given a sufficiently open mind and wallet—in just a weekend? We may even be told that the only thing that could prevent us from seeing the desired results from such a weekend is our lack of belief in the process. And so the shearing of the sheep goes on. Business as usual.

The greater our hurry to arrive where we want to be spiritually, the longer it will take. That which is spiritually greedy in us weighs us down as much as it revs us up, leaving us spinning our wheels while we look around for better deals. But in real spiritual hunger, there is no hurry and no wasting of time. When we are deeply immersed in spirituality, we are not time-bound, even as we take care of business in a timely fashion. The only spiritual shortcut is letting go of having any shortcuts. No rush. When we're on track, it doesn't really matter how long it takes to reach our destination, because we know in our heart of hearts that we are going in the right direction, however much the road might meander.

We pay so much for what we want and so little for what we really need. We want freedom for free. A man once asked the Dalai Lama how he could more quickly get to enlightenment and the Dalai Lama reportedly wept for him, recognizing how much pain that man had to be in to want to get enlightened faster. We think that "getting it" spiritually will give us immunity from pain and all the other troublesome matters of life—what a fantasy! Spirituality ultimately means no escape, no need for escape, and utter freedom *through* limitation and every sort of difficulty.

    When the desire to take a shortcut arises, enter the feeling of this desire to escape, moving beyond its mental dimensions until you are at its core, pressed against its primal pulse. There may be great fear here, but as you stay with it, cultivating intimacy with it and its existential concerns, it will mutate into more life-giving forms. Your very communion with such fear expands it beyond itself, until you come to rest in the feeling of Being, perhaps noticing that your flesh, so recently fearful, is patterned energy, wearing nothing but the attention given it. And with such essential ease, there is no hurry, no craving for shortcuts.

Gotta run. Busy day ahead. A pain in the neck, but still kind of intoxicating, keeping us so busy and so occupied that the mysteries of the obvious go all but unnoticed. But still something gets through the cracks in our sped-up, shortcut-craving days, undressing our spiritual ambition, asking only for our undivided attention and time. Awakening to a different mode of being, no longer desperate to have a shortcut because we are so grateful to be on our way, we smile with easy compassion at what we have done with our time, including our various detours into spiritual bypassing. The hourglass catches our glance, spinning into a flaming mandala of spilling forms (including our various selves), leaving a clearing that is everywhere at once, inhabited by a grace of which these words are but the feeblest echo.

BRINGING SHADOW WORKOUT OF THE SHADOWS

Shadow work—the practice of acknowledging, facing, engaging, and integrating what we have turned away from, disowned, or otherwise rejected in ourselves—is not significantly taken into account in religion and most spiritual paths, especially those that marginalize or insufficiently address the psychological and emotional dimensions of experience. (For the purposes of this chapter, I won't be discussing what is sometimes referred to as the "golden" shadow—the disavowal of our very best qualities, true size, and real nature—but rather the "dark" shadow and its less-than-flattering elements.) None of this is to say that religion and spirituality should be doing the job of psychology, but that they need to be more in touch with and supportive of practices like shadow work.

Schools of contemporary spirituality that are based in a more integral perspective take into account such realities as psychological repression and development, recognizing that there are some elements of our nature that spiritual practice may not be able to touch or significantly shift. As shadow work has become a more accepted concept (probably because of psychotherapy's widening cultural influence), it has begun appearing, however obliquely, on spiritual curricula in traditions that wouldn't have considered it not so long ago.

While this development might seem to indicate that spiritual bypassing is being addressed and outgrown, the concept of shadow work poses no problem to the more sophisticated varieties of spiritual bypassing. Superficial shadow work can easily have an illusion of depth; its superficiality may not be recognized even by its proponents. That we are occupying only the shallow end of the pool, safely removed from its shadowy depths, is easily obscured by the fact that we are actually in the pool. Yes, it is better that we are in the pool than not, but to mistake the shallow end for the deep end is just more spiritual bypassing—regardless of how wet we're getting.

And what exactly are shadow elements? They are the qualities and traits that we typically keep in the dark and project onto others, both at the personal and collective level, creating the very convincing illusion that such elements don't belong to us. Exposing this illusion and reclaiming the rejected elements of our being is the essence of shadow work. This practice asks a great deal of us, including an emotional openness and transparency that may be largely foreign to us. If we are genuinely engaged in such work, we will likely feel very uncomfortable at times, as old wounds surface and our sense of identity shifts in unexpected or challenging ways, perhaps asking for authentic answers to the question of who and what we actually are. Real shadow work does not leave us intact; it is not some neat and tidy process but rather an inherently messy one, as vital and unpredictably alive as birth.

The ass it kicks is the one upon which we are sitting; the pain it brings up is the pain we've been fleeing most of our life; the psychoemotional breakdowns it catalyzes are the precursors to hugely relevant breakthroughs; the doors it opens are doors that have shown up year after year in our dreams, awaiting our entry. Real shadow work not only breaks us down but also breaks us open, turning frozen yesterday into fluid now.

The first step is to wake up enough to see what is actually going on, and then to name it. For example, we have been angry at our partner for speaking unkindly to us earlier in the day and are now busy flaying him or her with invective for being so unkind, letting our anger mutate into aggression. We are raising our fist and pointing a righteously accusing forefinger, as if putting our partner on trial. If, however, we allow ourselves to recognize how we are cocreating these dynamics, we can, at least to some degree, interrupt and break out of our usual reactivity. And if we go a step further to name what we are doing—being reactive, hardhearted, aggressive, defensive, and so on, all projected onto our partner—we widen our view even farther. Now we have begun to illuminate our shadow.

The next step is to communicate what's going on for us, and to do so non-defensively. Vulnerability and transparency are needed here but, even if we can't be totally open, we can express our frame of mind, confessing our lack of openness. Admitting our feelings may be difficult, especially if we feel embarrassed or shameful for not having done things better or more skillfully. In fact, we might convert our shame so quickly into other emotions or states such as anger (directed at our partner or at ourselves), dissociation, or shutting down, that we render ourselves almost incapable of speaking up with any clarity or conviction.

But we can still communicate such difficulty if only through a pre-agreed-upon signal of some sort (like touching our mouth with our forefinger). The point is not to provide ourselves with an "out" or alibi for our sloppy behavior; instead of our partner backing us into a corner or confronting us, we do it ourselves. Yes, such self-exposure is often tough—and will likely bruise our egoity—but it is doable, and necessary if our relationship is to truly mature.

Although much of what we are facing is our own conditioning, the process of surfacing and working through it is for the most part relationally based. For example, in dealing with our reaction to what someone has just said or done to us, we may remember being treated similarly when we were young and suddenly find ourselves enmeshed in the past, slipping into whatever mode helped us cope with what was happening back then. When such deeply felt recollection possesses us in the midst of an interaction with another but we don't recognize that it is happening, we are in the dark. So what turns on the lights? Our own recognition of what we are doing, as perhaps signaled by a change in our voice or posture. Or the other person sees what we are doing and communicates it in way that we can hear. In either case, our shadow is brought out of the dark.

Yes, shadow work can be done alone, but it usually is more effective when engaged in supportive and skilled company. Thinking about our shadow elements, considering them from an emotionally safe distance, is altogether different than being in their cave, looking through their eyes, and breathing their breath. Getting up close to a particular shadow element is every bit as important as witnessing it and relating to it. This is often quite an emotionally rocky ride, especially given that we may find ourselves without our usual adult skills, at least for a time, because the wounded child in us has surfaced to such a degree that we are looking through those eyes and feeling those feelings. The key is to get as close as possible to that part of ourselves without getting lost in that old worldview, staying emotionally raw even as we name and illuminate what is occurring. When we skillfully meet our wounding and can understand its context, lucidly connecting our past and present, our healing is well underway.

Our shadow is then no longer in the dark. Courage deepens. Now the fire supplies not just heat but also light.

Emotional rawness and depth are essential to shadow work, both for ourselves and for those with whom we might be doing such work. If I haven't ever really raged about the abuse I suffered, how can I truly be present for your unleashed rage over the abuse you suffered? If I haven't cried deeply, what kind of environment can I provide for your deeper tears? If I haven't gone to the core of my fear, how can I really be with you as you go to the core of yours? If I haven't yet broken through to the root of my wounds, how can I expect you to do so in my presence?

None of this is to say that shadow work is easy to enter and practice! When shadow work is just beginning, there is, quite understandably, a reluctance to take it deeper; there frequently is too much investment in being right and/or comfortable, and too little in awakening to what is actually occurring. Not surprisingly, projection tends to runs rampant initially, much like it did between the United States and Russia during the Cold War. There is so much unexamined shadow material going on in—and running—us that our relationships are not much more than a no-man's-land wherein we skirmish for control or run roughshod over the other party, flag held high. A truly hollow victory.

Eventually, if we continue going more deeply into the work, our habit of distancing ourselves from shadow elements is replaced by a compassionate, courageous embracing of whatever we have disowned, marginalized, or rejected in ourselves. As we deeply encounter our shadow without losing ourselves in it, we free its energies and develop a genuine intimacy with it, until our shadow is no longer an "it" but rather a reclaimed us. This is true integration, organic and real, felt right to the core, manifesting as a deeply felt sense of wholeness, balance, and integrity.

The more deeply we dive, the less we mind upsetting waves.

What really matters is not so much the presence of our shadow side as the kind of relationship we choose to have with it. In spiritual bypassing we choose either to have no such relationship or to cultivate only an intellectual one, thereby keeping shadow work in the dark. How easy and how commonplace it is to turn away from what we don't like about ourselves, housing it so far below the surface that its cries cannot be heard, except perhaps as a distant echo. And yet its fists, its often tiny and so very young fists, continue hammering against the inside of our chest, calling to us, calling for us, calling for connection, illumination, love, and healing. All we have to do is enter what we have spent most of our life trying to escape or deny—a tall order, yes, but one that is definitely possible to achieve, step by conscious step.

Authentic shadow work does not allow cognition or spiritual realization to override, repress, or trivialize emotion (nor does it allow us to get lost in emotion or to devalue cognition). Identifying our inner critic is not the same as getting into the core pain that animates (and perhaps also legitimizes) our inner critic. Identifying and giving voice to various aspects of ourselves is useful, but to stop here keeps us stranded in a limited relationship with our depths. Going deeper means, in part, fully encountering and fully feeling our pain, entering and moving through it with open eyes and heart, becoming more and more intimate with it. Once we are well on our way to doing this, giving voice to a particular shadow element will no longer be from a "safe" or emotionally removed distance, and will therefore carry much more authenticity. Its cries will be our cries, its reaching will be our reaching, its rejection by us now just a piece of history, a souvenir of a more fragmented time.

Authentic shadow work includes all that we are, incorporating our physical, emotional, mental, spiritual, and social dimensions. To this end, psychotherapy is essential—not conventional talk-therapy (cognitive-behavioral, for example), but emotionally literate, somatically attuned, spiritually vital psychotherapy. Bodywork, intuitively and sensitively done in conjunction with emotional opening and therapeutic direction and insight, is highly useful in working with shadow material, not only because it works, but also because it usually works in a short time. (For more on the use of methodology in psychotherapy, see Appendix I.)

If our guides—be they spiritual teachers or psychotherapists—are not sufficiently familiar with the territory, not having done their own shadow work to a sufficient depth, they are not going to be at home with what their students or clients are doing, and so will probably cut off or marginalize such work (because it is triggering what is unresolved in them), usually without taking any responsibility for doing so.

When spiritual teachers who don't include any in-depth psychotherapy in their work claim to be doing shadow work with their students, they are simply doing their students—and themselves—a disservice. Their students are not being guided to the bottom of their pain; they are barely scratching the surface. Yes, there are spiritual practices, like some forms of "bare awareness" meditation, that can help bring shadow material to the surface while generating sufficient spaciousness in which to observe it. But as helpful as this can be, bringing meditatively rooted attention into such material is still not enough. We must fully feel our shadow side, and if the barriers we have erected to it are immune to spiritual practices like meditation, then something else is surely called for—and what a pity it is when the need for exploring different options, like psychotherapy or even a break from spiritual practice, is not honored.

May we not keep our shadow in the dark but instead become truly intimate with it, bringing to it a compassion that is both clear-hearted and disarmingly powerful, a compassion simultaneously fierce and tender, precise and far-reaching, personal and transpersonal. Such deep care helps transform our relationship to our shadow so that its energies serve rather than obstruct our well-being. Through this deepening integrity, we shift into a truer wholeness and open to a deeper life.

WHAT GENERATES SPIRITUAL BYPASSING?

Pain.

Or, more precisely, the avoidance of pain.

Pain comes with life, closely accompanied by our "solutions" to it, most of which are all about getting away from it, whether through alcoholic, narcotic, erotic, intellectual, material, egoistical, or spiritual means. The fact that these "solutions," despite their analgesic/anesthetic capacity, only end up catalyzing more pain usually does little to stop us from pursuing them.

Our resistance to our pain amplifies it. The more we try to avoid it, the darker and more tenaciously rooted it becomes. But when we stop avoiding our pain, when we cease judging or fighting it, its presence starts serving rather than hindering us. In turning toward and becoming intimate with our pain, we cut through our suffering—and by suffering, I mean the dramatization of pain—realizing not only that if we really want the treasure we will have to face the dragon, but also that our encounter with the dragon ensures we will be ready or sufficiently mature to truly appreciate and make good use of the treasure. As such, the dragon is not blocking our path; it is an essential part of our path.

When we are in the grip of spiritual bypassing we want nothing to do with the dragon, viewing it as a lower-brain roadblock, a vestigial negativity that is but a projection of old fears, while at the same time portraying the treasure, whatever it is, as ours as soon as we *believe* it to be—and so the treasure and the conceptualization of the treasure become conflated.

In spiritual bypassing's domain we are mostly marooned from the raw reality of our pain, numbing ourselves both to our deeper feelings and to the pain of others, disengaging to such a degree that our heart responds only superficially to even the worst sorts of pain. This is detachment, but not healthy detachment! In healthy detachment, we stand apart from what we are experiencing without disconnecting from it. But when we anesthetize ourselves to our pain, whether fully or in part, we are not in a position to really embody compassion, which leaves us with a primarily intellectual sense of compassion. However eloquently we may speak of compassion, universal love, equanimity, and other spiritual virtues, these tend to remain abstractions rather than fully embodied principles. At such times we are removed from the rawness of our pain, but not in a way that permits us to focus more clearly on what is actually occurring.

When we are caught up in spiritual bypassing, we want the treasure without having to face the dragon, believing that any negative thoughts or emotions require no more than waving our magic wand of positive thoughts and intentions to be conquered. The dragon, however, cannot be so easily pushed aside! It is so easy to get negative about negativity, turning away from our pain and whatever else reminds us that all is not well, regardless of our beliefs to the contrary. Turning toward our pain is an act of radical caring—and not just caring for ourselves—because in doing so we cease to fuel our avoidance and those addictive behaviors we have used to keep ourselves removed from pain. In turning toward our pain, we also, however indirectly, turn toward others' pain, both on the personal and collective level, (in both personal and collective contexts), and so our compassion for others deepens and widens. Turning toward our pain is about bringing into our heart all that we have rejected, ostracized, disowned, neglected, bypassed, shunned, excommunicated, or otherwise deemed as unworthy in ourselves. Our heart has room for it all. We are all faced with considerable challenges, not the least of which is our personal and collective conditioning. To be able to relate to our conditioning rather than simply identify with it is much more than just an intellectual undertaking, requiring that we turn toward and enter the very pain out of which much of our conditioning arose. And that turning toward, that courageous choice to become intimate with our pain and its roots, asks for much, much more than just a mere belief in or parroting of what we've been taught or read about our true nature. To emerge from our pain, we have to enter it.

The greater our fear of pain, the more extreme our spiritual bypassing "solutions" tend to be. We may, for example, present ourselves as having special spiritual status, on a continuum between grandiosity (inflated somebody-ness) and faux humility (inflated nobody-ness). This is akin to the excessive control often craved by those who grew up having far too little control. We may find ourselves very uncomfortable with the presence of others' pain, especially emotional pain, because it resonates, however quietly, with our own submerged pain, pulling it closer to the surface. When we are caught up in spiritual bypassing, our reluctance to acknowledge and feel our own pain keeps us standing apart from the pain of others, perhaps offering such spiritual bon mots as, "Tell me what you're getting out of creating this for yourself" or "It's perfect that this is happening" or "Stop living in the past" or, perhaps most commonly, "It's your karma." Anything to keep distance—plenty of distance.

Not all spiritual bypassing so blatantly avoids pain; the dance of avoidance can be done with great subtlety. Consider, for example, spiritual practices that advocate observing whatever arises with mindful attentiveness: these are not in and of themselves indicative of spiritual bypassing, but in the teaching to simply be an impartial witness to whatever is arising, there is a danger of becoming an overly passive or impersonal observer, thereby generating an excessive kind of detachment.

We might find a sense of reassuring comfort in doing such practices, which make a spiritual virtue out of standing apart from what is occurring, safely removed from any significantly close contact. Of course, this is not the fault of the practice but of how it is being employed and perhaps taught. As meditators, we may assume we are sitting with our pain—observing it moment-to-moment—when we in fact may just be sitting *on* it, using our witnessing capacity to keep it at a distance rather than becoming more intimate with it.

If a meditative technique is primarily used to avoid pain, spiritual bypassing is occurring. However, using meditation to ease pain or reduce its intensity does not necessarily signal spiritual bypassing but rather a kind of relaxation that allows us to enter more deeply into our life. Expanding our boundaries and softening around our area of pain gives it more room to breathe and stretch, more space to show itself in its various dimensions. Once our pain is a little less sharp, we can direct our attention into it, getting to know it from deep inside. The healing of pain is found in pain itself. Contrary to what we tend to believe, the more intimate we are with our pain, the less we suffer. Often when we say we are in pain, we are not really in our pain, but only closer to it than we would like. We are then in fact still outside it, still removed from it, still keeping our distance. By consciously and compassionately entering into our pain and cultivating intimacy with it, we begin to find some real freedom from our suffering. Our hurt may remain, but our relationship to it will have changed to the point where it's no longer such a problem to us, and in fact may even become a doorway into What Really Matters.

The point is not to romanticize the awakening power of pain any more than it is to bewail the presence of pain. Real freedom does not mean the absence of pain but rather fully embracing our pain without getting lost in its dramatics. This means fully facing whatever dragons are guarding the treasure we seek. And what are dragons but the archetypal presence of that which scares or appears to threaten us, not just from outside but from within? To reach the treasure we must face and encounter whatever dragons are guarding it.

In the beginning we may view our dragons—whatever shape they may take—as hindrances, problems, or inconveniences. Later on, however, we will come to view them not as obstructions on the path but rather as an essential part of the path. The path to what? To that for which we most deeply long. Establishing ourselves on this path means letting go of our suffering until there's nothing between us and our pain. This journey is ours to take. And if we choose to take it, we take it not just for our sake but for everyone's, as the more deeply we heal, the more of a life-giving force we become for others.

May we face our dragons and through our encounters with them find the healing, awakening, and freedom that is our birthright, realizing that our work is not to be freed from our pain but to be freed *through* our pain.

THE ANATOMY OF MAGICAL THINKING

Spiritual bypassing can be quite intellectually sophisticated, but sometimes (especially in its New Age forms) it finds expression through a far more simplistic form of cognition known as magical thinking.

Seeing causality in coincidence—giving unwarranted weight to coincidence—is central to magical thinking. Say we're driving along in a hurry and demand that the light up ahead turn green right away, and at that very moment the light turns green. Even though we know better, we connect our demand with the light turning green, sensing the juxtaposition of these two seemingly unrelated events as more than just a coincidence. This is magical thinking. We all have such moments, but sometimes these beliefs take deeper root, as in the proliferating New Age dogma that we have the capacity to radically alter our world through the power of thought.

Probably the most obvious form of magical thinking is superstition. How many of us avoid walking under ladders to ward off bad luck, or believe wearing clothes inside out brings good luck, or remain convinced that Friday the 13th is an ill-fated day? While we may know there's no logical justification for such beliefs, nevertheless we continue our rituals, with conviction and perhaps some degree of embarrassment. Who among us has not done something similar?

Magical thinking is a kind of prerational cognition. It is a mix of superstition, perception of illusory connections, and conflation of correlation with causation, attributing to our wishing, wanting, and imagining an inordinate power of manifestation. Hence the word *magical.* So if we as magical thinkers want something to happen, and if we want it with sufficient intentionality and focus, it will happen, or so we think, bypassing if necessary the laws of reality and other such inconveniences. (We do this quite automatically in our sleeping dreams, wherein our thoughts really do change or radically alter our dreamscape, often instantaneously.) If we only believe strongly enough, what we want will come about—or so goes the party line of "adult" magical thinking.

The idea of everyday omnipotence originates in childhood, when our sense of wonder and imagination are in full bloom. For example: a child is walking and notices that the sun is apparently "following" her; speeding up or slowing doesn't make any difference in the sun's positioning, so it is easy for her to conclude that the sun is indeed following along, much like a balloon on a handheld string. Or a child is crying and, seeing that it has begun to snow, attributes the coming of the snow to his tears. Or a child may believe that stepping on the cracks in a sidewalk will bring some sort of disaster or punishment. Such egocentrism, such a compelling sense that everything revolves around one, is developmentally natural for young children, but it is not natural for adults. Yet more than a few adults, including those caught up in spiritual bypassing, frequently think this way (even those who may claim to have transcended ego), and in fact make a virtue out of doing so, not recognizing the narcissism and superstition that animate their thinking. This mindset is especially common among spiritual practitioners who believe that if they concentrate their spiritual energies on what they want, they will have it. Of course, if they don't get what they want, this failure simply means that they didn't apply themselves sufficiently to the issue at hand. As childish as such thinking is, it is nonetheless astonishingly prevalent, particularly among those excessively attached to positive thinking, so-called prosperity consciousness, and spiritualized greed.

None of this is to say that there is anything inherently wrong with magical thinking. It is essential not only to our childhood and our early evolution as a species but also to our imaginative and dream-time faculties. But when we treat magical thinking as a literal rather than a metaphoric realm, we put ourselves in a difficult position, trying to fit reality into a box of our own devising. Magical thinking does not have to mean antiscientific gullibility or New Age hucksterism or the cognitive trump card of the densest sort of spiritual bypassing ("Can you prove that the spirit guide I see just behind your right shoulder isn't there?"). It can instead be a reality-reordering playfulness of mind, a life-affirming poetic license that takes its rightful place in our psyche, coloring but not animating our perspective. (Think of the sometimes startlingly original twists and turns of great poetry, which simultaneously employ and outshine magical thinking.) At the same time, though, magical thinking can be dangerous, such as when it is used to assert that those who are in dire circumstances have brought it on themselves. Those who feel they are responsible for their difficulties are less likely to seek the help they need because of the shame they feel, or the shaming they are receiving, for failing to visualize their way into a better situation.

Magical thinking can be very appealing to us—especially to the child in us—when we are deeply distressed, shocked, wounded, knocked flat by circumstances, or otherwise left feeling powerless. At such times, magical thinking presents an appealing direct promise of a pick-me-up of often epic proportions, intoxicating and distracting us with reassuring possibility, seducing us with nostalgia for the future. If this promise feels dreamy, it's because it literally is. A single thought in a dream can radically alter a dream's environment. Such is the seductive power of magical thinking. If we don't feel in control of our lives, magical thinking puts us back in control—or so it seems.

    None of this is to say that there is not a great deal of power in what and how we think; our thoughts may not literally create our reality, but they certainly can have a great impact on our reality. Anyone who has practiced lucid dreaming or highly intentional thinking knows how powerful and immediately impactful a single thought can be. But to attribute to a waking-state thought the power to *physically* alter our world in accord with what we're asking for is wishful thinking gone grandiose. Thinking that the sun is following us as we walk is obviously delusional, but so too is thinking that we "can have it all," that if we think positively enough about what we want, we'll get it.

Those who have extrapolated the well-known scientific fact that the observer (and the very process of observing) inevitably affects/alters what is being observed to help "prove" that our thoughts create our reality are confusing impact with outright creation. Yes, the observer is inextricably connected with the observed (and is not and cannot be in a position to be truly "objective") but he or she is not creating the observed—except perhaps in fantasies of omnipotence!

Our work is to relate to rather than from our magical thinking. Then we can see and feel its appeal and promises without getting sucked into them; we may even use magical thinking as part of our creative process, finding in it, for example, inspiration for our poetic leanings. But for those who are seduced by spiritual bypassing in its New Age garb, magical thinking is seen as a potent means to desired ends rather than the siren song of illusory power that it so often becomes.

But let us not be too tough on magical thinking, for even the wisest of us are likely to revert to it, however briefly, when certain conditions slam into us. When sufficiently wounded, disoriented, or out-of-control, we may find a certain solace in the sunny simplicity of magical thinking, in part because we have been flung back into the ways—now psychoemotional defaults—we learned to cope when we were young and suffering deeply. But fine as it may be to now and then spend some time in magical thinking's neverland, we need to treat it more as a stopover than as a place in which to take up residence, no matter how hurt or vulnerable we are.

Magical thinking relies heavily on "signs"—apparent clues, whether internal or external—that seem to point us in certain directions or to affirm something that we already intuit, giving us the green light to go ahead. In this, there usually is a mixture of superstition and intuition. We may, for example, be considering buying a car but be torn between a blue or yellow one; then we go into a bookstore to buy a couple books we've been looking forward to reading and see that the front cover of both books is predominantly blue, at which point we conclude that we are "meant" to purchase the blue car.

It's easy to laugh at this, but just about all of us engage in some form of this thinking at various times. A parking spot is just not there, so we may think that this means we should come back another time or shop elsewhere. Or we put on a jacket that we wore on an auspicious occasion as we head to a particularly important business meeting. Lucky charms, special pieces of jewelry, touching our front door twice as we are leaving the house, and so on—things with which we associate good fortune are given the power to positively impact our lives, especially when we strongly believe in them.

However absurd our superstition appears, it tends to help get us aligned with what we need to be doing, whether it's doing well at our business meeting, hitting big-league home runs, or emerging unscathed from a battle. Most of this is culturally accepted or at least tolerated. Rarely do we really mind that one of our favorite athletes "has to" wear a particular pair of socks to each playoff game; if it helps him do his best, and we want him to excel, then who cares if he's not thinking rationally? The point here is not to abandon superstition, nor to ostracize or muzzle it, but to recognize its presence as possibly signaling the presence of magical thinking, and therefore perhaps also spiritual bypassing.

Those of us who are heavily invested in signs are usually possessed by the belief that there are no such things as coincidences and that "everything happens for a reason." So if the bus is late, or if an apple falls at our feet, there must be some meaning in that for us, some sign. Part of the trouble with this is its opaque egocentrism—the assumption that this happened in order to teach *me* a lesson of some sort, which of course does not take into account all of the other waiting passengers and their needs, nor the state of the bus driver, nor the traffic delays or weather. No, it's all about *me*.

Maybe the bus is just plain late. And if the snowy conditions slowed it down, did that weather manifest just to teach me something? Yes, we can learn from everything, but not everything is arising in order just to teach us! We are just not that important; we are not that central. Magical thinking both makes us feel more significant than we actually are and reinforces the feeling of being part of something immeasurably vaster than us; while these may seem like positive things, they can buffer us from the impermanence and inevitably contingent nature of our existential condition.

A few minutes after writing the above paragraph, I watched a DVD with my wife Diane. It was one that I had never seen and knew nothing about, *Sleepless In Seattle,* and lo and behold, much of it was about, yes, signs! Coincidence? Maybe, but there are very few films that are so overtly concerned with signs, so …

So what about synchronicity? Is it—defined as the arising of meaningful connection through the encounter of causally unrelated events—just a branch of magical thinking, an assumption of connectedness that is in fact not really there? Not necessarily. Many a coincidence may actually be not a coincidence, but rather synchronicity—but this doesn't necessarily mean that all coincidences, all juxtapositions, are synchronicity in action. If I have a red pen in my hand and then see a red car driving by, there is no synchronicity, except perhaps to a prerational mindset.

But if I have a brand new, highly original idea that I've never spoken of to anyone and I go to tell you about it and find out, after having spoken only one or two words of it, that you have the very same idea already on the tip of your tongue, that is synchronicity. If I suddenly need a certain tool for a task, a tool I have never used before, and a friend who lives an hour away unexpectedly shows up with that very tool in hand, that is synchronicity. Many times when I have felt tired, clients have called to cancel their sessions that day—far, far more often than when I have not felt tired; the sheer frequency and clear meaningfulness of this indicates synchronicity. People showing up at just the right time to help; the almost-didn't-happen meeting of lifelong lovers brought together by the seemingly flimsiest alignment of circumstances; act of grace after act of grace—significant crossings all of these, occurring too often to be categorically categorized as accidents or mere chance. Synchronicity is not randomness in order's clothing or a misreading of coincidence, but rather a manifestation of the innate interconnectedness of life, occurring not just in prerational realms but also in rational and transrational realms.

Magical thinking cheapens synchronicity by elevating it to star status in New Age circles, using it to validate everything else that constitutes magical thinking—which makes the concept of synchronicity an even easier target for those who are already skeptical of it. Nevertheless, we can be free from magical thinking and still experience synchronicity, intuitively recognizing it rather than analytically concluding that it has indeed occurred. There often is a certain feeling (such as heightened sensitivity or a case of goose bumps) that accompanies synchronicity, a felt sense of obvious significance laced, however subtly, with a supramundane or numinous quality—revelation has become foreground, explanation background.

Those who employ magical thinking generally not only view it as something other than magical thinking but also usually are quick to point out the successes—financial, health-related, and so on—of those who conceptualize in this fashion. But how do we know that there really is a causal link between these peoples' magical thinking and the results they achieved? There may have been a positive correlation between the two, but this does not necessarily mean that magical thinking actually caused the aforementioned successes. If I wish and wish for something and it manifests, my wishing may have played a role in my success, but it was just one of many factors involved—and if we want to see what really caused my success, we are going to have to bring in everything that made it possible. After all, every apparent cause has its causes, and these causes have their causes, and so on, all bound together in a surpassingly complex contingency. Synchronicity is just part of a much larger realm of interconnection, occurring when two or more different aspects of the Whole get close enough to intersect and meaningfully resonate with us.

There is no need to eliminate magical thinking, but there is a need to keep it in healthy perspective, to cease allowing its prerational impulse to masquerade as a rationality-transcending mode of cognition. As long as we leave magical thinking unchallenged, we will remain in spiritual bypassing's grasp. Magical thinking is a souvenir of childhood; let's leave it there without, however, turning away from it, enjoying it in the same way that we enjoy spontaneous play and childlike creativity and fantastical films.

The irony is that as we leave magical thinking in the sandboxes of our mind, we don't have to become drearily serious grownups bereft of magic, but rather we can find a deeper magic, the magic of awakening beyond what we think ourselves to be. There is a remarkable innocence in this, not a naive or gullible innocence but a second innocence, a deeply awakened innocence through which our intimacy with the Mystery of Being ripens ever further, leaving us not longing for Home but sitting at the hearth, resting in the magic of the everyday, grateful to be here one more day.

WHY DON'T MORE SPIRITUAL TEACHERS INCLUDE PSYCHOTHERAPY IN THEIR WORK?

Quite a few spiritual teachers—with the notable exception of many in the Buddhist tradition—don't include psychotherapy, either directly or as something they wholeheartedly recommend, in the work they do with their students, even when it is obvious that the spiritual practices and teachings they prescribe are not working very well for some students, especially with regard to addressing their deeper wounds, needs, and psychosocial difficulties.

Rather than suggesting that these students engage in psychotherapy (and for the purposes of this chapter, I do not mean psychotherapy that is limited to talking and analysis, but that which also includes emotional opening and expressiveness, bodywork, and fitting spiritual practices, especially in integrative contexts, as described in Appendix I), such teachers typically recommend further spiritual practice, as if the only answer—or the only *good* answer—is to stay with the spiritual path they have prescribed. If fault is assigned for the student's lack of success on this path, it is usually placed on the student, with little or no fault attibuted to the spiritual teacher. (Such lopsidedness also frequently characterizes dysfunctional relationships, often generating a crippling shame in the student, rendering him or her less likely to seriously question or challenge a teacher.)

Spiritual teachers who view psychotherapy as something their students do not or should not need or, perhaps, as something to be done before entering spiritual practice, are doing their students a great disservice. These teachers tend to view psychotherapy as simply a reinforcer of egoity (and *personal* concerns) and therefore a distraction from more important things like spiritual practice. Not surprisingly, they see egoity as a hindrance to spiritual realization, an obstacle to be overcome, when in fact, the problem is not egoity but what we do with it. As increasing numbers of spiritual teachers and spiritually oriented psychotherapists are pointing out, ego development is essential to our maturation. Unfortunately, "ego" still has a negative connotation in many spiritual arenas—again, with the notable exception of much of contemporary Buddhism.

Another part of the reason why more spiritual teachers don't recommend psychotherapy for their students may be that they themselves have never undergone any psychotherapy or have had a negative experience with it. Spiritual teachers who state or imply that psychotherapy (and psychological work in general) is a lesser undertaking than spiritual practice—little more than wallowing around in one's personal history—are, however unwittingly, not only exposing their allegiance to spiritual bypassing but also shaming and spiritually bullying those students who really need psychotherapy.

I wonder how many who hold such a view possess a real familiarity with psychotherapy and its various schools and can distinguish—or are interested in distinguishing—superficial psychotherapy from the deeper stuff. And I wonder how many recognize that highly skilled psychotherapy is itself, without necessarily trying to be, often potently spiritual (as when it awakens as well as heals). More and more psychotherapists are employing spiritual practices and perspectives in their work—and in their personal lives—but are more and more spiritual teachers employing psychotherapeutic approaches in their work (and in *their* personal lives)? It doesn't appear so, beyond a few exceptions. Shadow work for some spiritual teachers is either viewed as a waste of time, a mere regression or "lower" activity, or as something to be approached only intellectually. Students who get stuck in very difficult states, states that their spiritual practices are not adequately reaching and addressing, are not directed to the resources that could help them most.

When I say we could really use more spiritual teachers who are also highly skilled in psychotherapy, I don't mean that all spiritual teachers should be psychotherapists (nor that all psychotherapists should be spiritual teachers)! But we do need more who are at home with psychotherapy, whether as actual practitioners or as well-informed advocates of it. Those who are not sympathetically aligned with psychotherapy and the need for it may easily misdirect their students who are struggling with issues like emotional expression and regressive behavior. To tell students that directly expressing anger, regardless of how it is expressed, is not a good thing, as some spiritual teachers (ranging from Buddhist elders like Thich Nhat Hanh to New Age positivity pushers) are inclined to do, is a disservice to their students, who may then muzzle and mute their anger in the name of spiritual correctness (especially if their early history predisposes them to do so), believing they are sitting with their anger when in fact they are just sitting on it.

The relationship between spiritual teacher and student can easily fall into codependency, unacknowledged parent/child transference issues, or even cultism, so cultivating and maintaining an awareness of potentially damaging dynamics is crucial, even in the best of settings. Doing so is made all the more difficult by spiritual teachers who lack psychological and emotional literacy and could really use some psychotherapeutic work, regardless of their spiritual attainments and access to exalted states. I'm less concerned about a spiritual teacher's access to such states than I am with what he or she is doing with them! It is very easy to confuse the attainment of such states with being at an advanced stage of spiritual practice and with being a truly mature (or deeply awakened and integrated) person. Students are usually quite easily impressed by such spiritual credentials, perhaps feeling some pride in being so closely associated with a spiritual teacher who has certain powers.

Yes, honor the transpersonal, embrace and abide in it, but not at the expense of the personal and the interpersonal! Everything exists through relationship, so why avoid any of it? Why avoid getting intimate with all that is? Why relegate the personal and interpersonal to a lower status than the transpersonal or transcendent impersonal? To avoid any of it is to remain incomplete, regardless of our spiritual achievements. Authentic spirituality is radically non-avoidant, recognizing that if we flee anything in ourselves, it will multiply and fester, enlarging itself to seize our attention, seeding its outcast will throughout us, eventually exposing and deflating our spiritual ambition.

Psychotherapy is often viewed as being just about learning how to function better (through clearly connecting the dots between past and present, adopting more skillful behaviors, and so on), but it is not just about that! Psychotherapy—and again, I am talking about body-including, emotionally literate, vitally integrative psychotherapy—is inherently spiritual, in that it invites in ever-deeper (and therefore more inclusive) perspectives, opens psychospiritual gates from the inside (at the optimal time), and asks the big questions (also at the optimal time), going for something more real than answers when necessary. Such psychotherapy is both a crucible and a sanctuary for needed healing, especially when combined with supportive spiritual practices. It begins with conversation and soon brings in whatever else helps deepen the work, including emotionally open dialogue between various aspects of ourselves, contextually attuned catharsis, and moving more and more fully into and through the heart of our pain. (For more on psychotherapeutic methodology, see Appendix I.)

Contemporary spiritual teachers who in their teachings and work don't include psychotherapy *and* who also act as if what they are presenting is, for all of their students, sufficient for spiritual awakening, are both deluded and dangerous. Yes, some students, a rare few, may not need any psychotherapy for their maturation, but their example should not be used to negate the vast majority who would surely benefit from adding some psychotherapy to their spiritual practices.

Some spiritual teachers may not want to incorporate psychotherapy in their work with their students because they fear that some students, perhaps many, might leave them if they were to do in-depth psychotherapy. Such teachers may claim that they have their students' best interests at heart, but in this they are more akin to parents who claim they have the best interests of their children at heart even as they overlook or marginalize what their children really need. Some students may need a move away from their spiritual community but fear that in doing so they will be labeled "wrong" or even "traitors" by those remaining in the group, especially if a leader frowns upon such departures or, at worst, frames them as betrayal. A mature spiritual teacher, however, allows his or her students to move on.

Spiritual teachers for whom integrity of the personal, transpersonal, and interpersonal is essential have far more interest in what is truly best for their students than in keeping them. These teachers don't object to their students doing psychotherapy and in fact will openly encourage it. They recognize that spiritual practices may not sufficiently address their students' conditioning and that other approaches, including the psychotherapeutic, need to be included, not to negate the spiritual but to augment and serve it. They recognize that an integral approach to healing and awakening is not mere theory but a deeply embodied, ever-evolving practice in which intimacy with all that we are is the curriculum and practice path.

This may be anathema to gurucentric spirituality, but it is balm and catalyst for the authentic spiritual path, in which students are fully encouraged to keep their critical faculties alive and well even as they surrender ever more deeply to the core imperatives of their being. In this approach, spirituality is awareness and love functioning as one, requiring no negation of—or separation from—the personal or interpersonal.

If as part of our spiritual path we were to choose intimacy over transcendence—including intimacy with all that we are—we'd be more at home, more deeply aligned with What Really Matters. This is precisely where psychotherapy needs to work closely with spirituality. After all, real freedom is found not in escaping limitation (one of spiritual bypassing's favorite fantasies!) but rather *through* limitation. In turning toward our limitations and allowing them to serve our awakening, we could not find a better team of allies than integrative psychotherapy and spiritual practice.

MAKING WISE USE OF ANGER

In spiritual bypassing's cosmology, anger is heavy-duty negativity, about as far from love and enlightened living as you can get; something that the spiritually advanced do not express (unless perhaps they are gurus doing it only for the "good" of their devotees) or, at best, even allow to arise. Getting openly angry—or even being angry—is considered to be spiritually incorrect in more than a few circles, especially in those that view anger as a hindrance or impurity (this being true of most of Buddhist teachings, for example). According to this thinking, anger is no more than aggression or hostile reactivity; it is something that needs to be converted into a "better" state, such as compassion. But, in truth, anger and compassion can coexist; wrathful compassion is not an oxymoron.

Plenty of meditators work at sitting with their "unwholesome" states, including anger, not realizing that they may not be so much sitting with these states as they are sitting on them. Repressed feelings don't go away just because we're now spiritual! In fact, they may get worse. Repressed anger is still anger and will find ways, however unangry looking, to surface, including through the ever-so-gentle judging of those who are more overt in their anger expression (of course, we may also judge others for their anger without necessarily having repressed our own). The fact that such judgment may be voiced very softly or nicely or reasonably does not make it any less judgmental or shaming.

It is so easy to trash anger. After all, when anger "possesses" us, are we not more prone to violence, ill will, hatred, and lovelessness? And even if we can somehow successfully counteract such possession, we have, it seems, done no more than curb the beast—it still paces behind its bars, fanged and all too eager to do damage, while we play vigilant zookeeper. Or, less commonly, we may romanticize anger, rationalizing our "natural" urges to uninhibitedly express ourselves in the name of emotional release and honesty.

In both cases, anger is treated as though it were an endogenous entity or mass, a thing either to be muzzled or set loose. Psychospiritual camps may argue the dangers of either letting anger out or keeping it in, but there is much more to working with anger than these either/or strategies would suggest. As we become more intimate with the anatomy and history of our anger, and as we learn to express it cleanly—that is, without blaming or shaming or aggression—its fieriness serves rather than hinders all involved by potently addressing behaviors and issues that are obstructing not just our well-being but that of others.

There is nothing inherently wrong with anger; it is not necessarily a problem—a sign of negativity or spiritual slippage, or an avoidance of something "deeper"—or a sign of not caring. It is how we use our anger that is the real issue. Let's look at how we relate to anger: Do we blame our anger for clouding or befuddling our reason—pleading victim to our passions being one of our oldest alibis—or do we assume responsibility for what we do with it? Do we turn our anger into a weapon, hiding our hurt behind its righteously pumped-up front, fueling and legitimizing our defensiveness with it, or do we instead keep it as transparent and permeable as possible, remaining vulnerable even as we allow its full, appropriate expression? Do we use our anger to get even, to score points, to overpower, or to out-debate? Or do we use it to deepen or resuscitate our intimacy with our partner, to compassionately flame through pretense and emotional deadwood?

It's so easy to reject, bad-mouth, crush, incarcerate, or otherwise violate our anger, allowing it so few life-enhancing outlets that, like an animal kept too long in a cage, it behaves badly when finally released, thereby confirming our suspicions that it needs the same treatment as a savage beast threatening our home. It is also easy, although less common, to glorify anger, with equally harmful results. Exhorting the inhibited to "get into their anger" may just lead to a forced anger of performance that leads not to healing insight but to an overreliance on simplistic (and possibly aggression-reinforcing) cathartic procedures.

It is, however, not so easy to cultivate intimacy with our anger. Getting close to its heat, its flames, its engorged intensity, without losing touch with our basic sanity, asks much of us. But if we do not ask—and ultimately demand—this engagement of ourselves, we will surely miss knowing not only the heat of anger's fire but also its light. As much as anger can injuriously burn, it can also illuminate; it all depends on what kind of relationship with anger we choose to cultivate. We can treat anger as an ally, an enemy, an inconvenience, a regressive activity, a resource, a means of aggression, or a means of deepening intimacy—it's our choice. We're not here to outgrow anger but to outgrow our dysfunctional ways of using it, and this begins with knowing anger well.

Anger is an aroused and often heated state that combines a compelling, strongly felt sense of being wronged (hence the *moral* quality of most anger) and a counteracting, potentially energizing feeling of power, both of which are interconnected biologically, psychologically, and culturally. It's also crucial to recognize that anger does not always outwardly manifest as what we normally would conceive of as anger. Can we identify anger—which is not a single emotion, but instead a family of related emotions ranging from annoyance to rage—through the observed presence of particular behaviors? Not necessarily. A person can display none of the behaviors supposedly characteristic of anger and still be angry. Instead of pounding the table or cursing the idiot who has dared to cut us off in traffic, in our anger we may instead try even harder to please our partner or smilingly withhold a piece of information that we know would help another. So, can we—or others—recognize our anger through observing our behavior? Again, not necessarily!

Similarly, can we identify anger through the observed presence of particular feelings? Two emotions, like envy and resentment, may feel very similar, having much the same physiological characteristics, yet they do differ. This difference is rooted in subjectivity—that is, in how we frame things. We discriminate between emotions by attuning, however unknowingly, to the context of the situation.

Because bodily sensations are usually so obviously involved in emotion, we may confuse them with emotion itself. There is, however, more to emotion than just the feeling of it. Anger is an attitude, not just a feeling. We evaluate emotion but not feeling—we may speak of our anger as "justified" or "unjustified," but would we say that our feeling like vomiting is "justified" or "unjustified"?

Also, we can cease being angry and yet still feel the very same feelings that only a moment ago we identified as anger. For example, as I am raging at you for scratching my new car, I find out from a trustworthy friend that you are in fact completely innocent; suddenly I am no longer angry at you. My evaluation of the situation has radically and almost instantaneously changed, yet the very feelings I was experiencing just a moment ago—pounding heart, facial flushing, shoulders knotting, hands ready to strike—are still clearly present, having diminished only slightly. So can I now call these feelings angry feelings? No, because their evaluative framework—or emotional basis—has changed. So it is very important not to confuse the sensations we associate with anger with anger itself. Even in its hot-blooded extremes, anger is as much a cognitive act as a feeling-based one, as is demonstrated by how quickly anger can rise or fall according to how we interpret a given situation.

It's important to realize that anger is not necessarily the same as aggression. Aggression involves attack, whereas anger may or may not. Aggression is not so much an outcome of anger as the result of avoiding our anger and underlying feelings of woundedness and vulnerability. Aggression is devoid of compassion and vulnerability, but anger, however fiery its delivery might be, can function in the service of compassion and vulnerability. Nevertheless, anger still remains synonymous with aggression in our culture, in both secular and spiritual contexts.

Viewing anger as aggression—or as the cause of aggression—gives us an excuse to classify it as a "lower" or "primitive" emotion, something far from spiritual. But while anger is far from primitive, what we do with it may be far from civilized! Anger that is directed to do injury, however subtly, is not really anger but hostility. Anger that masks its own hurt and vulnerability is not really anger but hardheartedness or hatred in the making, seeking not power *with* but power *over*.

Violence—aggression gone savage—ignores, tramples, or dynamites personal boundaries, but anger, in many cases, protects or guards such boundaries, at best resolutely exposing and illuminating (or perhaps even flaming through) barriers to intimacy or integrity without abusing those who are maintaining such barriers. Violence is not a result of anger but an abuse or violation of anger.

However, there is a potential healing here: to reverse the equation, to convert aggression, hostility, hatred, ill will, and every other diseased offspring of mishandled anger back into anger. This conversion does not mean eviscerating or drugging the energy of such negative states, but rather liberating ourselves from our constricting judgment about anger so that its passionate intensity can move freely and coexist with a caring, awakened attention. In this sense, the world needs not less anger but more—especially anger coming not only from the guts but from the heart.

The four approaches to working with anger, as introduced below, provide a framework for making sense out of the diverse, complex, and enormous amount of material concerning anger. This framework is sufficiently inclusive to cover both personal *and* transpersonal considerations of anger.

1. ANGER-IN refers to strategies favoring the restraining and redirection of the energies characteristic of raw anger. Not surprisingly, advocates of this approach emphasize the importance of *not* directly expressing anger. Self-control and the subduing of and recontextualizing our anger—these are the cornerstones of anger-in. Anger-in "experts" tend to equate the expressing of anger with "venting," a lack of self-control leading to violence and aggression. Though the anger-in approach makes a strong case for learning to step back from anger so that its more extreme or irrational impulses can be reconsidered or given more contextual space, it has a difficult question before it: How successful can a method of working with anger be if it does not include openly expressing the actual feelings of anger? Would we consider a grief therapy successful if it did not include the actual expression of grief?

2. **Anger-Out** refers to approaches that emphasize the importance of directly and fully expressing the energies and intentions of anger. At the very core of the anger-out theory and work is the notion of

catharsis, which remains a controversial topic in therapeutic practice, despite evidence that incorporating catharsis in anger-management work makes it more effective. Advocates of anger-out say that suppressed anger is not healthy—better to bring it to the surface (or "dig it up") and release or express it, they claim. As appealing and apparently medically sound as such down-to-earth logic may be, it can tend to overemphasize a merely physical approach to anger, as if anger was just something to discharge or eliminate from the body. The emotional-release work that character- izes anger-out practices can range from enthused license to blindly cutting loose (or irresponsibly "acted out" anger) to profoundly healing, integration-promoting release, and illumination.

3. **MINDFULLY HELD ANGER** refers to approaches in which anger is consciously contained rather than emotionally expressed, and

meditatively attended to with a key intention to neither suppress anger nor act it out. In its emphasis on neither repressing nor acting out emotion, this approach appears to offer a solution to the anger-in/anger-out dichotomy. In being wakefully present with our anger, thereby closely witnessing the actual *process* of it (in its feeling, cognitive, perceptual, and social dimensions), we also bear witness, at least to some degree, to the very "I" who is busy being angry. That is, our perspective shifts from how angry we feel to *who it is* who feels it. At its best, the mindful holding of anger is not so much a containment of anger as a deliberately intimate embracing and investigation of it, a willingness to stay with our anger without outwardly expressing it. However, this practice carries its own dangers—as suggested by the more negative connotations of the term "holding"—especially when it is engaged to flee or suppress anger. Those immersed in spiritual

bypassing tend to confuse this approach with that of anger-in.
4. **HEART-ANGER** refers to approaches in which openly expressed anger and compassion consciously and beneficially coexist. Put together the virtues of anger-in, anger-out, and mindfully held anger—healthy rationality and restraint, emotional openness and authenticity, meditative openness and compassion—minimize the difficulties associated with each, and heart-anger emerges. Heart-anger is anchored both in full-blooded aliveness and in clear caring for the other. As fierce as it sometimes can be, heart-anger is but the emissary of wrathful compassion. Here, the expression of anger is not necessarily rethought or kept to oneself, nor is it always given free rein. Rather it is deliberately infused with wakeful, investigative attention, without any requisite dilution or non-expression of its passion. Such anger has a broad enough sense of human suffering to embrace a radically inclusive

morality; it possesses sufficient faith in life to persist in its fierce caring; and it has the guts to carry all of this out.

Anger is moral fire. Whether it is destructive or constructive is in our hands ... and in our hearts. In the fiery care of clean anger, passion and compassion coexist, as do heat and light. We need to respect our anger, to cease viewing it as a problem, or a spiritual hindrance, or something beneath us, so that it might truly serve our well-being.

Anger that is denied compassion easily becomes anger delivered, however indirectly, without compassion. But how do we bring compassion to our anger? To neither repress nor indulge in our anger is a far from easy undertaking; the challenge is to meet our anger with mindfulness and genuine caring. First of all, we need to approach anger without aversion, which means becoming more intimate with whatever judgment we might have toward it. The degree of caring with which we approach our anger is the degree of caring we can bring to the anger we express to others. Not to explore anger, not to be intimate with it, is a dangerous choice, leaving us cut off from the positive potential of the very energies that can so easily become twisted into aggression, hatred, and mean-spiritedness. Not to know our anger is to keep ourselves in the dark, in danger of becoming aggressive or violent instead of simply angry.

At its best, anger—heart-including, open-bellied, open-throated, and passionately alive—can support love and integrity, for it is deeply connected to need, vulnerability, and the rawness of being. It becomes relational fire, helping to both clear and light our way into an ever-deeper intimacy that includes all that we are. The fiery intensity at the heart of anger asks not for smothering, spiritual rehabilitation, or mere discharge, but rather for a mindful embrace that does not demand any dilution of passion, any lowering of the heat, or any muting of the essential voice in the flames.

Bringing anger into our heart is not only an act of love for ourselves but for all beings, since such a practice increases the odds that we will not let our anger mutate into aggressiveness, hostility, and hatred but instead direct it toward compassion-centered activity. In no longer abandoning or destructively harnessing our anger, we move a step closer to standing up for the very love that we most desire from others.

How quickly and easily the heat of our preferences can stir up anger, while our mind, apparently uninvited, tosses in commentary: *Should I take my anger seriously? Should I wait until it passes? Should I express my anger directly, right now, or should I maybe reword it a little? Why is this happening to me? It is definitely your fault this time; why shouldn't I be angry at you? I guess my spiritual practice isn't what I thought—but would I be getting angry if you were treating me better? Observe the sensations and the intentions, inhale, exhale, inhale, exhale, inhale—damn, this just is not working! I promised myself I wouldn't lose control again, and here I am, already losing it—which would not be happening if you hadn't done what you just did, right?* And so on. Under such conditions, our thoughts are kerosene for anger's fire.

Where there are judgments, whether directed at ourselves or others, there is going to be anger. This does not mean that we somehow ought to get rid of our judgments—a bound-to-fail task, as long as we have a mind!—but rather that we keep them in healthy perspective, mining them for whatever nuggets of insight or intuition they might contain amidst all their noise and fuss.

It is not uncommon to be angry at our anger *(When will I be free of this damn anger?),* rejecting of it *(I shouldn't be angry!),* in denial of it *(You may think that I am angry, but I'm not!),* or simply disconnected from it *(I don't have any anger).* However, instead of fighting or fleeing our anger, we need to become more deeply acquainted with it. But how can we do this if we only examine our anger from a distance (anger-in), insist on emptying ourselves of its energies when it arises (anger-out), or, worse, pretend that it simply is not there? Intimacy with our anger enhances self-knowledge, integrity, relational depth, and spiritual maturation, helping us to embody a passion as potently alive as it is responsible, as we learn the art of being angry with an open heart.

The better we know our own anger and the more adept we are in expressing it, the more likely it is that we will be able to skillfully handle others' anger, but if we remain estranged from our own anger, not only will we express it sloppily, we will not be able to deal very well with others' anger. If we are on the receiving end of anger from those close to us, it may be very tempting to shut down—even if their anger is being delivered cleanly. We may interrupt, minimize, or try to deflect their intensity of feeling, perhaps informing them that they are out of control or behaving irresponsibly, saying to them in so many words, "Can't we do this another way?"

This apparently reasonable request, however appropriate it might be at times, is often a telling sign that we are far from intimate with our own anger, seeking to avoid it both in ourselves and others. Consciously or unconsciously, we worry that if we don't successfully defuse or mute their anger at us, it might catalyze our own anger into a more active form. The greater our investment in avoiding anger (even more likely if we are in the grip of spiritual bypassing), the more we will obstruct or sabotage it in others.

We may even demand that loved ones in the midst of their anger demonstrate that they do indeed love us—usually by asking that they stop being angry (or at least looking angry). As long as anger signals the end or absence of love for us, we are going to have a strong investment in suppressing it, both in ourselves and in others, thus stranding ourselves from the realization that anger and love can both exist at the same time.

Looking for proof that an angry significant other is not rejecting us can quite easily obscure the fact that we may be rejecting them and their anger. Demanding that they show us love (in the way that we think love ought to look) while they are angry at us can quite easily obscure the realization that *we* are withholding love in response, perhaps punishing them, however unwittingly, for being angry at us.

Our "calm" or "rational" or "spiritual" withdrawal when they are angry at us is very likely not an act of real caring but rather one of fear, aversion, or passive aggression. It is easy to make a virtue out of withheld anger, but such withholding may be just another form of anger. Part of our difficulty here may be that we are still confusing anger with aggression, forgetting that aggression-free anger helps protect our boundaries.

For anger to enhance intimacy, it needs to be met with non-defensive, empathetic listening (which does not necessarily mean that the person listening should suppress his or her own anger!) in which agreement or disagreement with what is being conveyed remains *secondary* to our empathy and caring for the other. Such is the essence of receiving anger. Rejecting a significant other's anger—not aggression, but anger—simply short-circuits it. This generally encourages the stockpiling of anger's energy and frustration, and creates pressure to find other outlets for it, such as erotic distractions, overwork, or the subtle cruelties of passive aggression.

Much as we might like to think otherwise, anger does not disappear as we evolve and awaken; in fact it may become even more fiery but burn more and more cleanly, clearing the temple of what does not belong there and serving the well-being of all involved. So don't make a goal out of bypassing anger at all costs. Aspire to something far more life-giving: a clean, conscious, fully alive anger, anger that both flames and bleeds, anger with heart.

BOUNDARIES MAKE FREEDOM POSSIBLE

Boundaries are an essential part of life. They delineate and maintain needed borders and separations, making differentiation possible at every level. Boundaries both contain and preserve the integrity of what they are safeguarding, be that physical, psychological, emotional, social, or spiritual. Without them there is no relationship and therefore no development, no evolution. But despite this clear truth, we often fall into the trap of believing that boundaries hold us back, preventing us from being free or realizing "nondual consciousness"—whatever untroubled, idealized state we may aspire to. If we thus equate having boundaries with being limited, and if being limitless is a cherished goal for us, we will tend to view boundaries as a problem, an obstruction to freedom, something to overcome.

Real freedom, however, is not about having no limitations; rather it is about finding liberation within—and also through—limitation (as when the apparent constraints of committed monogamous relationship actually enrich and deepen the relationship). Real freedom does not mind limitations and in fact is not limited by them.

Boundaries make freedom possible by clarifying what must be worked with, not just personally and transpersonally, but also interpersonally. Since everything—everything!—exists through relationship, it is crucial that we learn to work well within relationship, both with others and with our own needs, states, and identity. This work is not possible if our boundaries are not clearly delineated and skillfully maintained.

Whether our boundaries are collapsed, blurred, abandoned, trampled, disregarded, nurtured, overpoliced, cemented, or honored, they determine our edges, limits, borders. Boundaries may be overdefined, underdefined, or ambiguously defined. What really matters is what we do with our boundaries: Do we use them to fortify our ego or to illuminate it? Do we lose ourselves in them or hold them in healthy perspective? Do we use them to keep ourselves from love or to deepen our capacity to love? Do we concretize them or do we keep them flexible? Do we allow them to be overly permeable or do we allow them to be as solid as circumstances require? Do we use our boundaries to isolate ourselves or to create and deepen connection? Do we employ our boundaries as guardians or as guards?

These and related questions are important to consider, and to keep on considering—we need our boundaries, and we also need to keep a clear eye on what we are doing with them.

Without healthy boundaries, we cannot have healthy relationships.

Without healthy boundaries, we stunt our growth.

So what are healthy boundaries? They are steadfast guardians, serving both to contain and preserve the integrity of what they are safeguarding. Boundaries don't just hold space; they make and honor space by keeping it appropriately compartmentalized. They keep particular aspects of us enclosed until they are sufficiently developed. A premature rupturing of self-encapsulation (as when we are forced into adult responsibilities when we are young children) interferes with our development, leaving us with leaky or otherwise dysfunctional boundaries.

A healthy boundary is a psychophysical presence—a kind of energetic membrane—possessing the necessary firmness to protect us from invasion, intrusion, violation, and other dehumanizing or life-negating forces, as well as the resiliency to soften and open to what is beneficial for us. For example, we may hold a boundary regarding others' anger; if their anger is hostile or mean-spirited or sarcastic, we keep our boundary firm, without apology, but if their anger is clean, being free of blaming and shaming and aggression, we can allow our boundary to be more permeable, letting in their anger and whatever message it carries because this feels safe to us.

Healthy boundaries serve our highest good. They are akin to the loving parental hand that holds our hand as we take our first child-steps along a seaside wall or a playground ramp, gripping us neither too tightly nor too loosely. That touch, so reassuringly solid and steady, gives us the courage to venture farther afoot. As we mature, we will find that some of our boundaries can be expanded or made more permeable; for example, if we have an intimate partner, we can expand our boundaries to include him or her rather than collapsing or ignoring our boundaries in order to be close. Such expansion does not weaken our boundaries any more than expanding our love weakens it.

Healthy boundaries serve our evolution. Each developmental stage is fittingly nested in a cooperative complex of boundaries, holding us so that we can, as optimally as possible, navigate the terrain and learn whatever is needed (this process, of course, is often obstructed by factors like poor parenting or traumatic events). If we are overboundaried, we'll stay too solidly put, remaining stuck in significant ways, with only part of us moving on (as when we keep developing cognitively but not emotionally or morally). And if we are underboundaried, we won't stay with a particular stage long enough or go deeply enough to learn what we need to from it, thereby becoming little more than developmental dilettantes, touring rather than really living out particular stages of growth. Without healthy boundaries, we don't grow; we age but don't really evolve. Healthy boundaries set us apart without separating us and bring us together without homogenizing us.

If we are inclined to be overboundaried—overbudgeting for defense—we wall ourselves in, confusing security with freedom. On the other hand, if we tend to be underboundaried—leaving the gates too open—we float on the periphery of embodied life, confusing fusion with intimacy, limitlessness with freedom, and excessive tolerance with compassion. Boundaries make containment possible, but does such containment protect or overprotect us, entrap or serve us, ground or cement us, house or jail us?

Those who are underboundaried tend to mistake collapsed boundaries for expanded ones; especially in the realm of spiritual bypassing, a collapsing (or outright dissolution) of boundaries is seen as letting go of or even transcending them. A similar mistake is made in our idealized view of romance, where the overwhelming urge to merge is seen as the ultimate state of love rather than as a temporary fantastical state that inevitably unravels over time. We may rationalize or glamorize this abandonment of boundaries as a kind of liberation, a casting-off of shackles in the service of transcendence and spiritual realization. As much as we might conceive of such radical expansion as a wonderful thing, confusing our flight from boundedness with true openness, we don't realize that the actual practice of spiritual bypassing does not expand boundaries but rather neglects and disrespects them. For example, someone we are close to speaks very disrespectfully to us, clearly crossing a line, and instead of asserting ourselves with them, taking a needed stand, we leave their behavior unaddressed and unchallenged, thinking we are being compassionate with them, thereby disrespecting our boundary that was inappropriately crossed.

Abandoning our boundaries is not indicative of a higher or more noble state—however much we might spiritually rationalize this—but is just escapism and aversion, an avoidance of facing, entering, and moving through our pain. Dissociation in spiritual robes is still dissociation! We may make a virtue out of moving beyond the personal, perhaps thinking that we are transcending it, when in fact we are slipping into the domain of depersonalization (a well-known psychiatric disorder featuring disconnection from one's sense of self). But depersonalization is not the same as the self-transcending or "no-self" realizations of advanced spiritual practice! It is just another form of dissociation (or unhealthy separation).

What is arguably the opposite of dissociation? Intimacy. And intimacy requires healthy boundaries. Healthy boundaries protect but do not overprotect; they stand guard but do not jail. If we keep ourselves overprotected, we don't thrive but stagnate. And if we keep ourselves underprotected, we also don't thrive but open ourselves undiscerningly, left in a state in which over-absorption is inevitable. The spiritual bypasser in us might protest: shouldn't we be receptive? Yes, but overabsorption and receptivity are not necessarily the same thing! Consider the example of a man who is exaggeratedly nice and almost always smiling, even when he is treated badly. He may appear very receptive and unusually open, but in fact he is taking in much more than is healthy for him, perhaps because this strategy—never saying a clear "no"—helped him survive difficulties in his early years.

Having healthy boundaries doesn't mean a lack of receptivity; instead, it is a discerning receptivity, an openness that can just as easily say a full-blooded "no" as a "yes." The undiscriminating openness and too easy "yes" (and possible show of equanimity) of those who are underboundaried is especially difficult to cut through when it's taken to be a sign of spiritual attainment. When we cannot voice and embody an unequivocal "no," allowing ourselves to be closed at times, our only way of protecting ourselves is to dissociate, to get away from what's difficult rather than face and pass through it.

Where being overboundaried appears to promise freedom through security, being underboundaried seems to promise freedom through limitlessness. But both cut us off from living fully. This fact is usually obvious when we overprotect ourselves but not necessarily when we underprotect ourselves, especially when we legitimize our actions spiritually, making an unquestioned virtue out of our undiscriminating openness. For example, we may open our sexual boundaries in the name of universal love, reframing our multi-partnered sexual encounters as tantric practice, thinking we are being more openhearted than those "stuck" in monogamous relationships, since they, unlike us, are limited to just one partner. While our true nature is indeed limitless, the way in which it manifests in this world, in individual form, is necessarily equipped with boundaries. Boundaries may seem to divide up that which is undivided and whole, but it is through such division that a deeper, more integrated whole is created, in much the same way that cells, through their very division and differentiation, make tissue and organs—and an embodied us—possible. We cannot hope to mature and find true integration without first being clearly differentiated, vividly and unmistakably outlined. Good boundaries provide and support this essential differentiation in our lives.

The primary emotional state that functions to uphold our boundaries is anger—which is quite problematic for those who view anger as a merely negative state. This view is especially common in Buddhism, which (with the exception of Rinzai Zen and Tantric Buddhism) generally conceives of anger as no more than an afflictive or unwholesome state, confusing it with aggression. Classic Buddhist texts generally take a very negative view of anger, seeing no value in it per se (other than as something to transform into compassion), and much of contemporary Westernized Buddhism follows suit (with the notable exception of teachers like Jack Kornfield and the many psychotherapists who are Buddhists), not bothering to distinguish anger from aggression, confusing anger with what is actually done with anger, and advocating that practitioners not express anger, all the while failing see that compassion and openly expressed anger can coexist.

Those enmeshed in spiritual bypassing rarely see any value in anger, being too busy avoiding it to recognize its value and function as an energetic guardian of our boundaries. We tend to try not to look or act angry, even when we are raging inside, turning away from the very forcefulness and fieriness that empowers us to properly enforce our boundaries. Without free access to our anger, our "no" lacks the intensity (however quiet it might be) and strength to have the impact it needs, and our "yes" remains anemic, cut off from real vitality. Those who can't or won't say a full-blooded "no" and stand firmly behind it frequently find themselves in situations that require a clear "no," like the people in the 2009 Sedona sweat-lodge tragedy. Not having the voice and energy to assert the boundaries we need leaves us at the mercy of forces that may be detrimental to us.

Boundaries allow differences to play their essential role by preserving our autonomy and making healthy interrelatedness possible—a fact clearly illustrated in mature relationships, in which there is deep communion without any dilution of one's sense of self. In such relationships, we don't discard our boundaries to make meaningful connections; we expand our boundaries to include the other without short-changing ourselves. Such inclusion has room not only for shared love and joy but also for shared pain; both partners are able to hold compassionate space for the pain of each. When we are caught up in spiritual bypassing, our aversion to all that is painful and uncomfortable tends to keep our relationships superficial. It is so easy to allow our misguided embrace of our intrinsic oneness to separate us from our differences!

Imagine a place with no pain, no judgment, no nasty moral dilemmas, a place where whatever happens is just karma, just the perfection of Being unfolding as it must. Imagine not just visiting there or dreaming of being there, but actually dwelling there. Such is the narcotic promise of spiritual bypassing. This is a dream not to fulfill but to awaken from. Of course we yearn for freedom, for real transcendence, but we need to have something from which to take flight. Healthy boundaries provide the ground for stable footing. Spiritual bypassing, however, uproots us before we've established such ground, mostly through its devaluing of the personal and interpersonal in favor of "higher" realities, and its accompanying neglect of boundaries. Along the way, relational intimacy is left mostly by the wayside, as if it were little more than some vestigial practice for those misguided souls still trying to have a worldly relationship free from spiritual ambition.

Boundaries make intimacy possible in a number of ways. Yes, relational intimacy is really just Being meeting Being through the medium of form, but at the same time it is also individuated being meeting individuated being, mixing and sharing differences, generating a kind of hybrid vigor and evolutionary richness through doing so. Relational intimacy can be a very potent path to awakening, equally honoring the one and the many, but those of us whose spiritual bypassing manifests through estrangement from intimacy have cut ourselves off from this path, having made ourselves all but invulnerable to its demands.

We are not here to shed or abandon our boundaries, but to breathe integrity and strength into them, to fully illuminate them, and to make sure that they take a form that serves not only our highest good but also the highest good of all. We are not here to override or devalue our boundaries but to use them as wisely as possible, valuing the personal and interpersonal as much as the transpersonal, and discovering the freedom in fully engaging our experience. Our boundaries stand as guardians on this path, with an authority that supports our growth and awakening.

DON'T TAKE IT PERSONALLY?

The separate self—the seemingly autonomous "I" or personality of everyday experience—is not looked upon with much favor in some spiritual circles, probably because so many of us over- associate it with ego. This "I" can manifest at one extreme as narcissism or excessive self-concern (a tempest in a me-knot), and at the other extreme as healthy, full-blown individuality. But no matter how mature this "I" appears, it may still be viewed as an obstacle to spiritual realization by those overly enamored with the concept of oneness, resulting in a devaluing of the personal relative to the spiritual.

Spiritual paths that overvalue and cling to the notion of transcendence tend to pathologize ego, seeing it as no more than something that has to be overcome or eradicated if we are to spiritually awaken—and so "I" is treated as no more than an incarnational tagalong of a decidedly lower vibration, at best adding a bit of color and flair to the proceedings. While less depersonalized spiritual paths may acknowledge the value of individuation and personality, they may still too readily conflate these with ego, encouraging us not to take things personally since doing so might entrench us in ego-centered responses.

Depersonalized spirituality is an anemic undertaking in which hollowness is confused with transparency, ungroundedness with altitude, flimsy boundaries with openness, and emotional flatness with equanimity. When we're in its grip, we usually don't bother differentiating between egoity and individuality, keeping ourselves busy fueling and marketing the Oneness Express and the Transcendence Monorail, preaching the gospel of nonseparation even as we advocate separating from or getting rid of ego. We may, if we are caught up in spiritual bypassing, be psyched about the notion that everything is all One, but when it comes down to being one with our "lower" qualities like our anger or greed, we much prefer cutting ourselves off from them, even as we pay lip service to their being one with everything else.

Such a demoting of—and disengaging from—individuation, especially its passionately alive, deeply engaged aspects, is central to spiritual bypassing, constituting not freedom from "selfing" (the process of generating a sense of self) but a refusal to fully develop and embody a self, to individualize. Yes, our sense of self or personality can itself be observed, demonstrating that our true identity lies beyond it, but such observation is not of much use if we employ it to withdraw from or marginalize the personal.

No matter how we treat it, our personality persists. Some of it evolves and some of it doesn't, successfully resisting every remedial program, spiritual or otherwise, that is aimed at it. Once we are on our way to cutting through our spiritual ambition, we realize that although there is no need to transform our personality, there is a need to learn to relate to it rather than just to identify with it.

This does not mean, however, that we have to distance ourselves from our personality and its quirks but rather that we need to cultivate just enough separation to bring it into clear focus, at which point we can develop an intimacy with it. In this way we become consciously close to our individuality, holding it with lucid compassion without fusing with it.

In such radical subjectivity, we can allow our individuality to show up in all of its personalized colors so that it exists as a nonbinding, deeply idiosyncratic expression of who and what we truly are. The more at home we become with our individuality—knowing it and its origins intimately—the more skillfully we can navigate it and our relational and spiritual dimensions as well, giving each its due, allowing all three aspects of us—personal, interpersonal, and transpersonal—to fruitfully coexist, without letting any one of them assume or usurp the throne of self.

We are advised by many spiritual authorities not to take things personally, and many of us have bought into this admonition without really looking into it. It is an attractive notion, simple and seemingly commonsensical, implying a certain detachment, even immunity, which allows us to keep our cool and not spin off into reactivity. Reminding ourselves that whatever is coming our way from others is not really about us, but rather about them, helps us not to get knocked off center but has the unfortunate side-effect of distancing us from the fact that sometimes what is coming our way from others *is* about us to some degree—and therefore needs to be taken personally with, of course, as much consciousness as possible.

Spiritual bypassing is often characterized by an insistent emphasis on not taking things personally. It is, after all, usually easier to take things *impersonally,* if only because we are so detached that we don't have to get emotionally involved. Plenty of what passes for healthy detachment is far from healthy, reflecting an attachment to being detached, to maintaining enough separation from what is happening to not have to really feel it.

Not taking things personally can be an illuminating and eminently practical practice, allowing us to respond sanely to difficult circumstances, but it carries a hefty shadow comprised of dissociation, depersonalization, and disconnection. There may be a premature leap from labeling "my" traits to "the" traits when we have done little or no in-depth work on a particular quality or trait. For example, we may have considerable fear, but rather than investigate and become truly intimate with it, we skip to the distancing (and supposedly more spiritual) language of referring to it as "the" fear rather than as "my" fear; in this way, we have not embodied or genuinely arrived at a transcendent view of reality but have simply disowned our fear. Once we have become intimate with our fear, however, knowing it from deep inside, we can legitimately relate to it not just as "my" fear but *also* as "the" fear. There is no dissociation in this—just a capacity to see and work with fear primarily as a psychoenergetic phenomenon, level upon level, along with an expansion of our boundaries to include collective fear.

If our beloved suddenly dies, and well-meaning friends or family advise us not to take it personally, what does this do to us? We're far better off not listening to their advice and taking our beloved's demise personally—very personally—letting the bare reality of it go right to our heart, feeling our way into and through our shock and denial, allowing our hurt to stream as wildly and deeply as it needs to, with no apology for how profoundly and painfully personal the situation feels. We are taking it personally, but in doing this so fully, so totally and consciously, we are also opening ourselves to the essential mystery of things without trying to prematurely establish ourselves there. That is, we are taking it personally, while also taking it interpersonally and transpersonally.

"Don't take it personally" can be good advice under many sorts of conditions, but it ought not to be applied to everything. A discerning eye is necessary. Some situations call for us to take them personally, to let them touch and impact us deeply. This is not the same as falling into reactivity, however. If a particular situation calls for us to take it personally, this does not mean to overpersonalize and dramatize or get lost in it, but to let it impact us without taking us over. This is perhaps best done in the spirit of good parents tending to their just-injured child; yes, they deeply feel for their child in an obviously personal way, but at the same time, they cultivate just enough distance from what is happening to be able to take good care of their child.

Beyond the rigidity of making a virtue out of not taking anything personally is the possibility of responding intuitively and discerningly to whatever comes our way, sometimes letting it in, sometimes not, without allowing a sense of spiritual correctness to determine our reaction. In this way, we experience no unnecessary separation, no clinging to detachment, no immunizing against pain—just openness, at once boundaried and boundless, drawing us not away from our humanness but into its heartland.

RELEASING SEX FROM THE OBLIGATION TO MAKE US FEEL BETTER

For the last forty or so years, we have been living in a pervasively sexualized culture—the word *sexy* has been used to describe just about every dimension of life, to an absurd extreme. While there's much more openness regarding sex than there was fifty or sixty years ago, most of that openness has more to do with breadth than depth; all too often we are undiscerningly open yet closed off from a truly vulnerable intimacy. While we have much more permission to experiment with sex and talk graphically about it, we rarely talk about it in real depth very often—exploring, for example, the *nonsexual* dynamics that may be in play during sex—for to do so would put us in a position of real vulnerability and transparency, in which we could not hang onto a semblance of "having it together" as easily. Seeing what we may *really* be doing while we are being sexual is likely not very high on our list of priorities.

The misuse of sex, particularly through the expectations with which we commonly burden it (like making us feel better or more secure), is so culturally pervasive and deeply ingrained as to go largely unnoticed, except in its more lurid or blatantly dysfunctional extremes. Even more removed from scrutiny is our aversion to exploring and illuminating sexuality in the context of our entirety, our inherent wholeness.

People so often crystallize sex out and apart from the rest of their experience. Rather than focusing on the mechanics of sex, we need to instead embody it with everything we do and are so that as much as possible, sex is not just an act of specialized function nor an act bound to the chore of making us feel better or more secure, but rather an unfettered aspect of *already* present, already loving, already complete expression.

This era of so-called informed consent is centered on the myth—yes, the myth—of consenting adults. In sexual circumstances, many of us may not be clearly considering what is really going on and what is at stake, instead making choices from a desire (largely rooted in childhood) to get approval, affection, connection, love, or security, or to be distracted from our suffering. At such times, we are operating not as consenting adults but as *adult-erated* children whose "consent" is but an expression of unresolved woundedness or unmet nonsexual needs.

Saying "yes" from a conditioning-driven consciousness is totally different than saying "yes" from an awakened consciousness aware of its conditioning, but if we have a hormonally driven investment in hearing "yes," then we won't particularly care where it comes from. And if our "yes" to going ahead sexually is spiritualized—framed as something sacred—then we will probably be all the more tempted to proceed.

Spiritualized sexual practices—generally operating under the rubric "tantric"—are very much in vogue, typically being taken to be good for us and even liberating, freeing us from the constraints of conventional sexuality, transporting us into zones where sex and spirituality juicily coexist, unburdened by the boundaries of everyday sex. Or so we are led to believe. Those who promote tantric sex view it as a higher or more evolved form of sex, a sacred interplay, often overlooking the considerable distraction it may provide from whatever unhealthy underpinnings might be present in our sexuality.

Not surprisingly, more and more people claim to be practicing—or at least to believe in—tantric sex. To state that we are tantric with our sexuality confers on us the status of having outgrown conventional sexuality, achieving the status of being spiritually sexy—we used to just have sex, but now we are practicing tantra! We may still have sloppy or flaccid sexual boundaries, but now we can rationalize this by reframing it not just as openness but as *spiritual* openness.

When those who promote tantric sex do not recognize to any significant degree the nonsexual and presexual forces that may be driving sexuality, they tend to overvalue what they are promoting, unwittingly encouraging a bypassing of what really needs attention. Those who were sexually abused as children can easily use not only everyday sexuality to continue acting out the core dynamics of their abusive past but can also use tantrically framed sexuality for the very same purpose, bypassing their unresolved abuse issues with spiritually sanctioned erotic rituals and beliefs, replaying their abuse while at the same time finding some degree of pleasurable distraction from it through the feel good capacity of sex. And those who weren't sexually abused as children but were abused in other ways—physical and verbal violence, heavy shaming, serious neglect, and so on—can also use sexuality, both in secular and spiritual contexts, to simultaneously act out the dynamics of their past and discharge some of the very tension generated by such replaying. When gripped by our conditioning, it is so easy to eroticize our unresolved hurt and unmet needs, all the while assuming that we are simply being sexual.

We may think that our sexual charge with a particular person is no more than an expression of our natural sexuality when it may actually be an eroticizing of our conditioning or of some nonsexual need we have. For example, the sexual arousal that a man feels when fantasizing about being longingly gazed at by an attractive, completely available naked woman may only be *secondarily* sexual, with its primary impetus being rooted in his longing to be unconditionally seen, loved, and wanted by his mother. Another example is that of a woman who, having had an emotionally unavailable father, is attracted to a man who is also emotionally unavailable. She finds herself magnetically drawn to him—and also drawn to making him want her (she felt she never got her father to really want her, but the charge to have this happen has remained with her). She feels strong sexual chemistry with this new man, enough so to obscure, at least for a while, the reality of his emotional distance from her. She has eroticized her charge of being with a man who is not emotionally available to her, distancing herself from her capacity to reject such an unhealthy involvement.

Just because we don't say "no" to a particular opportunity, sexual or otherwise, does not necessarily mean that we actually want to go ahead with it. I've seen many women in psychotherapy who could not initially say a real "no," because when they had originally needed to say it (usually as young children), they were in a situation—usually featuring some sort of violence—where it was far too dangerous to say "no." They had learned, for reasons of pure survival, to shut up. Would they say "no" to a man who was sexually interested in them? Not directly. Not even if he were repulsive to them. Once they had reclaimed their real voice and power, however, they could readily voice and stand behind their "no," making no apologies for their boundaries.

Those with firm sexual boundaries may sometimes be shamed by others for not being "freer," as if such boundaries are only signs of sexual repression, uptightness, moral rigidity, or simply barriers to sexual freedom. But those who advocate the free exchange of sexual energy with others, including in supposedly spiritual contexts, may actually be more entrapped than their more boundaried counterparts, caught up as they are in sexually acting out old needs to be unconstrained and to have more control over their interactions with others. In the undiscerning openness of much of spiritualized sexuality, the eroticizing of unresolved issues (like craving being wanted or craving being in control) becomes confused with real sexual freedom.

When we reroute the energetic charge (whether positive or negative) that we carry from unresolved past issues into the pleasuring possibilities of sex, we move away from the pain that underlies such excitation—the very pain that, if consciously entered, can help awaken and liberate us. At such times, the energetic release we find through sex robs us of—and distracts us from—the very energy we need in order to enter, explore, and work through our unresolved past issues.

It is crucial that we not exclude the exploration of our conditioning (and its eroticizing) from our sex life—and at the same time, it is crucial not to overestimate or glamorize the awakening power of sex. Engaging in tantric sexual practices can serve our well-being and it can also delude us, especially when we use such practices to override or bypass our pain and less-than-healthy qualities. As long as we can manipulate others for our own ends and frame our dysfunction as something else entirely, we are only screwing ourselves, regardless of whatever justification, tantric or otherwise, we give our behavior.

You cannot have sexual maturity without a corresponding emotional, moral, mental, psychological, and spiritual maturity. Those who are very developed intellectually but whose hearts are not open will not be sexually mature, tending either to be shut off sexually or to indulge in erotic fantasy. Those who are relatively advanced spiritually but who lack emotional intelligence will also not be sexually mature, tending to emotionally disconnect during sex or to burden it with tantric expectations. And so on. None of this, however, is to say that sex cannot be spiritual—for it can be, in mind-blowing, astonishingly illuminating, and ecstatic ways. Sometimes the first profound spiritual opening we experience is during sex, often without any forewarning.

Sex-as-sensation has come out of the closet—both in mundane and spiritual contexts—but not sex as radically intimate responsible passion, needing no manuals or maps, conventional, postmodern, tantric, and otherwise. The deepest sex—sex that requires no fantasies (inner or outer), turn-on strategies, or rituals of arousal, but needs only the love, openness, transparency, and integrity of awakened intimacy—cannot be experienced without a corresponding depth in our relationship with our partner. Without such mutual maturity, it doesn't matter how hot or juicy or innovative or tantrically informed our sexual life may be.

To reach sexual maturity, we need to face and deeply explore the less-than-mature ways we have employed our sexuality, usually as a means of making ourselves feel better. High up on the list is the eroticizing of our needs, which means both to sexually frame them and to seek their fulfillment—or at least something resembling their fulfillment—through sexual activity. We can eroticize just about anything from our past that we still have a charge with, plugging our original excitation (however negative) around the experience into sexual channels, thereby simultaneously reliving it—however indirectly—and finding some temporary release from it.

Our sexuality is often little more than this kind of eroticizing. Some men, for example, may think that they are extremely sexual—wanting to have sex a number of times every day with their partner—when in fact they are not really very sexual at all, but are simply overloaded with anger or fear, so much so that they find considerable energetic release, however brief (and however unknowingly) of that anger or fear through their sexuality. Ejaculation is their release valve, their fast-fix depressurizer, and their partner is little more than the outlet for this.

Likewise, some women who make a show of being sexually open are in reality very insecure and have found increased security by presenting themselves as overly available. They have just eroticized—and, in some cases, also spiritualized—their need for security, as demonstrated by having power over men (having perhaps been overpowered by their father or other males—or even other women—when they were little).

Consider a darker example: A man frequents sadomasochism parlors, getting the most sexual pleasure out of being whipped. In his fantasies, he associates sexuality with violence and is drawn to porn that features this association. Some might think he's just sexually kinky (and also perhaps that what he's doing is fine, as long as it's between "consenting" adults), but what's truer is that he's deeply wounded. Take away the erotic overlay in his fantasies and practices and what's left is violence and a gaping lack of love. It's no big surprise to find out that as a boy, he was severely beaten almost daily by his mother and that that was the only touch he got from her. Eroticizing his internalized and unresolved violence simply took the edge off the trauma, but stripping it down to its roots made possible a healing that quickly eroded his interest in sadomasochistic porn and practices. Once the original pain had been openly felt and skillfully worked with, there was no longer any need to sexualize it.

Some erotic fantasies may be quite complex, but their themes are not. Such complexity might in fact just reflect a need to have many things in order or under control so that the longed-for outcome can occur, a need that likely has its roots in circumstances that were dangerously or painfully out of order or out of control in our early years. But whatever their details, our eroticized needs are just that—needs. Strip them of their erotic overlay and presentation, and what remains is what is not yet healed. Once we realize that the eroticizing of our needs and unresolved wounds is both an escape from suffering and a mark of it, we put ourselves in a position where we can free our sexuality from the obligation to make us feel better.

In so doing, we are not only taking charge of our charge—embodying a newfound responsibility for the arising and amplification of our sexual charge—we are also no longer keeping sex in a headlock, be it pelvic or tantric. Thus do we enter sexual integrity. To de-eroticize our needs and wounds is to see them in their rawness and to turn toward what we really need.

Real sex does not promise joy, it *begins* with joy, with ease, with love, and with uncensored intimacy, needing no spiritual trappings for its unfolding. Let us cease using our sexuality to distract us from our suffering. Let us come to it *already* open, already happy, already connected—and no longer sentencing it to slave labor in the sweatshops of our neuroses. If sexual passion does not arise out of mutual love and connection, then why force it? Why try to induce it? Why fantasize or try to spiritually vault ourselves into it?

Sex can be profoundly spiritual when we stop attempting to engineer it into "higher" domains. All that's needed is deeply shared trust, love, transparency, and full-blooded commitment to what truly serves both us and our partner. Then sex becomes love in the ecstatically intimate raw, a succulently sacred, emotionally naked dance of passion and grace that expresses and celebrates already-present connectedness.

NEITHER ROMANCING NOR FLEEING RELATIONSHIP

When we're entrenched in spiritual bypassing, we tend to like our relationships sunnyside-up: No confrontation, no anger, no messy feelings, nothing that leaves any egg on our face. Smiles and relentless gentleness often dominate the relational menu, with everyone doing their best to make nice. There is not just denial here; there is also considerable dissociation, perhaps masquerading as spiritualized detachment and equanimity. Such relational disengagement maroons us from the vulnerability and depth needed for real intimacy, leaving us in psychoemotional flatlands.

But the opposite can also happen when we're caught up in spiritual bypassing: Instead of there being just a flight to dissociation, there may be a flight to fusion. Personal boundaries may become sufficiently weakened or marginalized to the point of dissolving differences between partners. Such fusion, whatever its romantic trappings, does not demonstrate true union or intimacy; instead it demonstrates a kind of interpersonal homogenization. So our relationships may be dominated by dissociation (unhealthy separation) or by fusion (unhealthy connectedness)—two sides of the same dysfunctional-boundaries coin, with the former passed off as nonattachment and the latter as communion or intimacy or "oneness." Such fusion, however, signals not that our separateness has been transcended but that it has been marginalized; our boundaries have been collapsed rather than expanded, and the distance between us has not been truly crossed but rather skipped over and denied.

Just like in conventional romance.

When fantasy-centered excitation grips us emotionally and when we confuse fusion with communion and intimacy, we may find ourselves in a romance packed with swooning idealism and runaway hope, enthusing about union and true love. Although many of us recognize the folly of such a romantic union, plenty of us still wish for it, believing it to be a lovely thing, an essential part of love, when in fact it is not love at all but an intoxicating cocktail of eroticized idealism and hope. Spiritualizing this notion makes it all the more enticing, infusing us with "meant-to-be" signs and notions that only further blind us. At the same time, however, getting romantically entangled may be a step that readies us for authentic love, if only by rendering our heart raw enough to yearn for deeper, more grounded connection.

Romance is a deliciously edgy dream, happily feverish and therefore not easy to wake up from, but wake up from it we must if we are to live in genuine love, the kind that makes real intimacy possible. When we are in the grip of romance, we tend to feel swoony, off balance, and intoxicated, marooned from our critical faculties and immersed in our cozy bubble of apparent intimacy (a cult of two), unaware of the rude pricks of reality that our very situation is inevitably attracting. Eventually, as passion loses some of its intensity and doubts creep in, the dream's fabric thins, and lovers start wondering where they went wrong, failing to see that what is not working in the relationship has been there all along.

Just about anyone can get romantic, but far fewer people can truly love and sustain love. Romance asks little more of us than popping a pill, but love—especially love in genuinely intimate relationship—asks for plenty, requiring not just our hearts but our wakefulness, our integrity and discernment, and our capacity to both open and protect ourselves. Cutting through our romantic illusions does not, however, mean an end to relational magic; rather it means grounding our relationship in mutually awakened, truly intimate interrelatedness. Romance drugs us; love awakens us.

Another reason why we tend to prefer romance to love is that romance can so potently distract us—at least for a time—from that which is painful in our lives, whereas love asks us to bring what is painful into our heart, no matter how much that might hurt. Romance turns away from the more challenging aspects of life, but love turns toward them. This is not the idealized love of spiritual bypassing but the love that is the animating force of true intimacy.

To further clarify the romancing of relational "oneness," let us consider neonatal "unity"—which in much of spiritual bypassing is commonly equated with nondual, enlightened consciousness, as if the newborn and the sage are in the same state. The world of the newborn is one of near-seamless cohesiveness, in which everything is part of an unbroken whole. Space, time, and causality are not yet experienced as such; we go not from here to there, but only from here to here—and from now to now. Such unity is not always blissful, but even if it contains disturbing elements, it is still a universe without boundaries.

It can be tempting to romanticize this apparent oneness of very early infancy, as though it were a lost paradise, comparable—or even identical—to the enlightened state of sages. However, the neonate's being exists *prior* to differentiation—boundaries have not been transcended or dissolved; they have simply not yet developed. For the sage, on the other hand, differentiation has gone so far that all aspects of self have been fully experienced and recognized to be none other than Being. That is, the sage has not collapsed his or her boundaries but rather has expanded them to include all. It is a radical embrace, as conscious as it is real.

The sage has transcended dualism, whereas the newborn has yet to enter it, not having awakened to the fact that he or she has been born into a realm of deeply ingrained dualism, a world far from awakened. And enter dualism the neonate eventually must, losing his or her unified state in the process, just as lovers immersed in a romantic swoon must sooner or later suffer the intrusion of the very forces for which their fusion was a remedy and face the reality of their differences. While we may see the neonate's entry into the world of duality as a fall from paradise, it is a necessary learning process in which the formation and presence of limitations and boundaries—and our relationship to these—is precisely the path to a true realization of nonduality.

The excitation-generating collapse of personal boundaries that characterizes romance might seem to recapture some of the numinosity and lost glory of the neonatal universe, but it actually just obscures the distance and incompatibilities that *already* exist between the romantic duo. When that distance can no longer be denied, we may feel as if we have been booted out of paradise, but in fact we are being given an opportunity rich with potentially liberating disillusionment, an opportunity to do the work that makes possible a deeper, romance-transcending, love-rooted life.

In romanticizing the dissolution or shedding of personal boundaries, we are highly prone to overlooking the hazards of doing so, which range from cultic enmeshment to full-blown psychosis. We may also forget that the neonate does not yet have boundaries to dissolve and that this little being we are glorifying is profoundly and utterly helpless. How eager are we really to recapture that unparalleled helplessness, fragility, and utter dependence? Or are we, in our romanticizing of the newborn's world, simply looking for some sort of immunity from our exaggeratedly dualistic, fragmented, inevitably painful and disappointing world?

Spiritual bypassing in relationships tends to manifest as spiritually rationalized avoidance of true intimacy not only through dissociation or fusion—as we have seen—but also sometimes through making a virtue out of overemphasizing one's own responsibility for problems that arise, in the spirit of believing "I create my reality." In this paradigm we are encouraged to consider what any difficulty we are having in a relationship says about us, and us alone, as though what our partner has said or done does not need to be addressed at all. While we may believe that casting a critical eye on another's behavior is simply a way to avoid looking at ourselves, not allowing ourselves to be critical is in fact an avoidance of relational interplay and depth, if only because of our spiritually correct resolution to not make any upsetting waves.

So if I say something critical (read: judgmental) about what you have done or are doing, all you have to do is let me know that my criticism is really about me, at which point I am supposed to examine what I've just said to you says about me. That is, our tacit task is to turn all the heat back onto me, with no resistance on my part. This helps us avoid confrontation—and, along with it, our chance to communicate in a truly honest and deep way. So while our relationship may look deep—because we are being so "spiritual" about it—we're actually just trapping ourselves in practices that keep things nice and safe (read: dissociated) from the vitality, passion, and messiness that come with true intimacy.

If I say something critical to you about what you've done or are doing, there is another card you can play to keep us "safe" from any sort of heated exchange—you can let me know that I am just projecting onto you. If I say that I am not projecting, you can simply let me know that I am in denial, reminding me that whatever we don't like about another is really only about us not liking the very same quality in ourselves You can, in short, shame me, however indirectly, for being so deluded as to think that what is going on is about you, not me. And on it goes.

Yes, sometimes when we are in conflict we will project our own shortcomings or darker elements onto our partner, but what about the times when we are not projecting, when he or she really has crossed the line? In a healthy relationship, there is ample room for confrontation, anger, and emotionally raw vitality. There is room for gut-level honesty, both with ourselves and with our significant others; it's a mutual commitment to blowing the whistle on ourselves without, however, cutting others too much slack. Instead of rising above or otherwise avoiding our difficulties, we go into and through them together, finding in such mutual voyaging and sharing an ever-deepening intimacy.

When caught by spiritual bypassing, we tend to romance rather than live reality—and nowhere is this more evident than in our relationships, where our fear of intimacy can become neatly and nicely spiritualized into an idealization of detachment or overmerged unity. So let us become as intimate as possible with our own spiritual bypassing tendencies, going beneath the surface to the fear at their core, and discover the awakening potential of true intimacy, which allows us to connect without fusing and to stand apart without dissociating.

Freedom through intimacy.

DISEMBODIED SPIRITUALITY AND EMBODIED BEING

When we are in spiritual bypassing's grasp, we usually tend—like James Joyce's character, Mr. Duffy—to live a short distance from our body. This is true even if we are doing things like yoga, meditation, or regular gym workouts. We may associate to varying degrees with our physicality, putting it through its paces, but we usually do not really inhabit our body; we spend most of our time only in its uppermost chamber—our *head* quarters. But even there, we rarely consider questions such as: Is the body just the mind's way of conducting business? Is it merely a container for the ego or soul? Is it simply an assembly of tissue, bone, and blood? Or is it something more?

When I see clients who are out of touch with their bodies getting more embodied (especially through deep emotional work in conjunction with meditative grounding practices), they move more gracefully, act more as a whole than as an assemblage of poorly connected parts, speak with more resonance and presence, and have a brightly alert yet settled quality to their eyes. Put simply, they feel more real, both to themselves and to others. Getting more embodied is a very tangible undertaking!

Having an affair with embodiment is not the same as being in an intimately committed relationship with it. Keeping our distance from our somatic reality is not just something we do when we are caught up in spiritual bypassing; it is a commonplace habit that pervades our entire culture, as epitomized by our chronic overabsorption in our mental dimensions—that is, being "in our head." While living this way might appear to be a perfectly natural and appropriate case of "mind over matter," it is in fact a culturally normalized flight from embodiment that relegates the body from the neck down to an "it" with which we've been saddled. A long history of body-denying spirituality, both Western and Eastern, has only reinforced this negative mindset, along with the idea that the body is but a container for who we really are.

To be truly embodied is to be intimate with our body, to know it from the inside structurally, emotionally, and energetically—and to know it with more than our mind. For many of us, though, this may be a far from appealing practice. After all, if we go deep into the body we will likely encounter some unpleasant feelings and sensations from lingering, unresolved wounds, and what, we may ask, is the point of going there? It's so much easier to mentally distance ourselves or even dissociate, especially if we can frame doing so as some sort of spiritual practice.

Instead of learning to embody ourselves, many of us have learned to disembody ourselves: to be in our head, to live from our mind, to overvalue cognition and undervalue feeling, losing ourselves in abstraction, spiritualized and otherwise. Picture a vast area of open ocean upon which bob countless head-sized buoys, each one personalized—an expanse of floating heads, bodies below the surface, unseen. This image—too close to home to be granted postcard immortality—represents much of the state of our collective awareness regarding our physicality. It invites us to consider some serious below-the-surface reflection.

So often we merely tolerate the body, dreaming of transcendence, of dwelling in higher states of consciousness beyond our physical form. Of course we are more than our body, but our body is an integral expression of who and what we truly are. We must beware the tendency of disembodied spirituality that views the body as a karmic burden, a price to be paid for incarnating rather than as something to value, an essential aspect of our nature through which we can truly awaken.

Of course, our secular culture has long perpetuated the mind-body split, privileging the mind over the body. Vast though the cultural obsession with body image may be, our core fascination is with the body as an object rather than as a vital expression of our being. Treating our body as an "it" either to exploit for its pleasuring capacity or to turn away from when it disappoints us keeps us disconnected, anchored more by beliefs and abstraction than by body-centered, body-honoring experience. Consider the conventional uniform of business, in which the ubiquitous tie—a far from functional item of clothing—clearly separates head and body, existing as a tightened noose around the lower part of the neck, cutting off much of the energetic flow between head and torso. Such psychoemotional decapitation pervades more than suit wearers, however—and how could it not, given the lopsided focus on intellectual development in our schooling system.

When we depict aliens, we typically give them oversized heads; their bodies seem almost an afterthought. Is this not a kind of collective self-portrait, an unwittingly accurate picture of the alienation we have visited upon ourselves? We imagine more advanced beings as ones of vastly expanded brainpower, with bodies little more than luggage for manifesting on the visible plane. And is not spiritual bypassing itself an alienating practice, abducting us from our full humanity and capacity for down-to-earth embodiment?

But no matter how much we might neglect or mistreat it, our body calls us back through its aches and pains and imbalances to take real care of it, to integrate it with the rest of our being, to honor and love it, and to recognize it as an expression of who and what we truly are. It is essential that we rediscover and treat the body as an inherently sacred expression of our fundamental nature, and that we outgrow our dissociative tendencies and judgment about body image. Somatic idealism has done incredible damage to us, as exemplified by the unending obsession with how we—and others—look. Until we get under the skin of our distorted body image, journeying into and through its psychological origins, we will be at its mercy, held hostage by its ubiquitous mirrors. "The flesh" has been slapped with negative press for millennia, being associated with sin, carnality, moral weakness, and disease. Many of us don't seem to like our body very much, or we may like it but not want it to change, as it inevitably must. In either case, we are burdening our body with unrealistic expectations, central among them our obsession with not showing signs of aging. Our body not only reveals what's going on for us emotionally—through its posture, gestures, expressions—but also signals our impermanent nature, no matter how much we try to stave off change through endless exercise, diet, or plastic surgery. If we don't want to be reminded of our mortality, we are going to keep our distance from our body, despite the attention we may seem to lavish on it. So what's a body to do?

As consciously as possible, bring awareness—compassionately wakeful attentiveness—into sensation, into emotion, and into the energetic patternings and psychological holdings of the body. Moving toward and into emotion, feeling it in the raw and giving it room for expression while understanding its connection to events in our life, is an especially effective way to reconnect with the body. We may be resistant to doing this, given that there might be considerable pain and perhaps also trauma embedded in the deeper layers of emotion, but in contacting and freeing up such zones of feeling, we become more integrated, more intimate, with our body.

In looking at our body, we may find ourselves looking down upon it, and not just geographically. But is it really "down there"? Is our belly really below us? Our legs? And if so, from *whose* point of view? When we view our body from the vantage point of our cranial headquarters, it may very well seem as if we are above it, when in fact all we have done is separate our head from the rest of our body, with our neck caught in between. No wonder so many of us have neck problems! When I do handson work with clients' necks during psychotherapy, it usually doesn't take long for them to experience much more of an energetic flow between their head and torso, often accompanied by considerable emotional release and insight into what is giving them a "pain in the neck." Reducing the body to the status of a concretized "it" is somatic estrangement—and if we are thus estranged, out of touch with our own body, we are going to have great difficulty relating with sufficient sensitivity and ecological savvy to our collective body, the body of Nature, regardless of our philosophy. Our tendency to talk about our body as a separate entity reveals the pervasive nature of our mind-body disconnect: "It" gets sick, old, infirm; "it" isn't attractive enough, healthy enough, strong or resilient enough; "it" betrays us, embarrasses, and disobeys us. In short, "it" brings us down. The litany continues—the body is unpredictable, unreasonable, too hot or too cold, too tired or too wired, too thick or too thin, too this or too that, constantly demanding to be filled, then emptied, then filled and emptied again, again and again making trouble.

The very "I" for whom the body is just an "it" may successfully masquerade as the real us, but it is just an assembly of habits in the habit of referring to itself as "I," a personified interiority that has been allowed to squat on the throne of self. This "I" acts as if it is a tenured indweller, but it is little more than a cult of one, however rational it might seem. Because of its lack of somatic anchoring and attunement, this "I" is poorly informed about our basic needs. And given its estrangement from feeling, it tends to be dry and overly abstract, typically favoring the intellectual over the experiential, the dispassionate over the passionate, the objective over the subjective. Regardless of its smarts, disembodied rationality is too committed to mental inquiry to have a genuinely beneficial impact on any significant scale. It is too busy dissecting and categorizing to have any intimacy with the messy, raw feelings and emotions that might taint its sterilized sanctums. Such rationality is really an irrational rationality, disconnected as it is from somatic and emotional reality. We need to stop looking up to such rationality, lacking as it does the ground from which to cast an integrated eye on anything. There is a wisdom in the body, a wisdom in feeling, that when accessed and allowed to operate in conjunction with our cognitive capacities leads to a deeper, wiser, more integrated life. So we need to get back to the body, which involves much more than just dropping it off at yoga classes or fitness facilities or medical offices. We can get our body more flexible, more fit, and more powerful, and we can load it up with the finest supplements and organic fare, and still be out of touch with it. Getting back to the body means doing whatever is needed to cut through our disembodied experience, which in part means a journey into and through the very pain that first drove us to disown and dissociate from our body.

The first step is to name this pain, to openly acknowledge the reality of it. The second step is to turn toward it, however counterintuitive this might seem to us, so that we are directly facing it, and the third step is to enter it, getting beneath its surface and encountering its originating dynamics. In so doing we become not only more intimate with our pain, but also more intimate with our resistance to entering our pain. As we engage in this process, we find ourselves more and more immersed in our somatic reality, with a considerable deepening of both our sensory and emotional awareness. We feel more deeply—feeling into, feeling for, feeling with—becoming increasingly present to our body. Instead of just thinking as we walk, we become more aware of the actual process of walking, enjoying the sensory flow and particulars of our experience. We may still feel much of our old pain, but now we can hold it in a way that catalyzes its healing.

Getting back to and into the body does not mean abandoning our intellect but rather allowing it to synergistically coexist with the social, somatic, emotional, spiritual, moral, aesthetic, and survival dimensions of intelligence. Getting back to the body is not a backward step; it is an opportunity to return to a full-blooded embodied now, a now centered not by ego but by intrinsic awareness, a now in which the personal, interpersonal, and transpersonal are in fitting embrace. Such multidimensional yet grounded presence is a common experience when we go toward, enter, and pass through our unresolved wounds, as I have seen countless times in my work over the past three decades. Getting back to the body means closely examining our assumptions about our body. Consider, for example, the notion of literally being "in" a body. To assume that we are actually "in" a body not only reduces the body to a container, a housing project, a thing, but also implies an out for us, an exit, a potential escape or getaway. After all, how could we even consider going out of the body if we didn't already believe that we were in it?

We cannot, however, go out of the body because we are not actually "in" a body. Who we are makes its appearance not in a body but *as* a body. This does not necessarily mean that we literally are our body, but that our body expresses rather than contains us.

You might ask: So, what about out-of-body experiences (OOBEs)? Does not their existence prove that we are in a body? Not necessarily. They simply show that substantial disconnection from the physical is possible at times other than when we're sleeping. We don't then so much exit from the body as let the body exit from us; we are conscious but not consciously embodied. The sense of separation that characterizes OOBEs may be simply that, a sense of separation or tangible apartness, perhaps triggered by the settling of attention in zones of the brain that are ordinarily activated through intense shock or extreme stress. Quite a few clients who endured horrendous abuse as children have said they watched their abuse from somewhere close to the ceiling or off in a corner, splitting off from their body as a pure survival mechanism.

An essential part of becoming more embodied is not just witnessing but feeling our body, both externally and internally, with unmuddied attention, not from an intellectual or compartmentalized distance, or from a supposedly higher or ascended consciousness, but directly, letting awareness and sensation fully meet. To really feel our body is an art in which compassion, patience, and the spirit of exploration all coexist. Here we meet spirit in the flesh, spirit-as-flesh, and discover the profound mystery and functioning of the soul incarnate. In this, our physicality is but an expression, a unique shaping of the source of the body, resonating with What Really Matters, giving us a means through which to relate to all that is. As such, embodiment is the ultimate participatory act.

The body asks only to be loved, lived, and illuminated. It is not some rigidly separate, self-existing mass but is continuous—and not just elementally—with all that is, at essence being but precipitated Being, spun from gravity and boundless light. The body is not just matter! (And for that matter, matter is not just matter.) The body is not a burden with which we've been saddled, nor is it an obstruction to realizing our true nature. Whatever its wrapping, our body is a gift. We need to shift from having a body to being a body, and from being a body to Being. In permitting a fuller, saner embodiment of our essential nature, we make possible a deeper life for ourselves, a life in which we cannot help but breathe integrity into our stride, and develop a deep intimacy with all that we are.

We tend to take embodiment itself as a given, failing to recognize its hyperbole-shattering import and beauty, its evolutionary imperative that makes possible healing, transformation, and homecoming. Allow intrinsic awareness to tour and explore your body until it is obvious that your body is not really yours but is sentient energy on the move, in concert with all that is. We must not only love what outlives this body but this body also, for it is a unique flowering whose rise and beauty and singularity ache to be known before its demise.

Whether or not we listen to its messages—as articulated through its structuring, gestures, tensions, and emotionality—our body is always revealing not just where we have been but also who we are busy being moment-to-moment. The damage—and not just physical damage—we have done and have had done to ourselves remains eloquently present in our body, however camouflaged it might be by the compensatory twists and turns we may have taken, unless we've done some deep healing. Such work is necessarily deep and emotionally raw at least some of the time, inviting us to shift from frozen yesterday to fluidly grounded now.

The memory of what crippled—and *still* cripples—us waits in our cells, our tissues, our organs, and our fascia and skele-tomuscular tensions, fresh as at the time it was first imprinted upon us. The trouble is such memory is not primarily lodged in our everyday awareness; its presence there usually has been long stripped of its emotional depth in its translation from the depths to the surface. Memories of emotional depth are found in seemingly less-accessible zones of our interior.

Just as we, as a collective social body, have to now store enormous amounts of radioactive waste in firmly sealed, densely walled receptacles, so too does our body have to store or contain—and keep as far away as possible from our everyday consciousness—whatever traumatic imprints it has not been able to release. (*Secondary* releases—sexual and otherwise—may make us feel a bit better, but only briefly and superficially relieve us of the "outer" stress resulting from the pressure and rising presence of underlying trauma.)

Storing pain that cannot be handled at the time is not just something that we do; it's a survival strategy that goes way back. Consider the amoeba: Put it in water that's been polluted with India ink granules, and it will actually absorb and store them in vacuoles (tiny self-contained cavities in the protoplasm of a cell). Then put the amoeba in water that's clean and its vacuoles will move to the edge of the cell membrane—like surfacing trauma in a healthy therapeutic setting—and discharge the ink granules.

Our capacity to isolate and encapsulate trauma so that the rest of our system can function adequately continues to amaze me. What is truly remarkable is that the very containment of trauma, however neurotically managed and compensated for, has permitted organismic and personal survival. We may have to "eat" it, we may have to swallow it, we may have to act as if it's not tearing at our insides, but we do not have to *digest* it. Our "vacuoles" aren't literal containers—though they may appear to have specific bodily locations—but rather inner mechanisms that make possible the repression of pain, especially unbearable pain.

We may, quite understandably, be very touchy about being touched in our areas of trauma. Our tightly constricted abdominal muscles, for example, may resist any significant softening or letting go because then we'd be closer to feeling whatever initially made—and is still making—such contraction necessary. Or such muscles may be too loose or too soft, offering no resistance to outside touch, as if uninhabited or vacated, indicating how we originally protected ourselves. In either case, our needed healing involves the body, especially in its emotional dimensions. Our desire to stay as far away as possible from our pain fuels our bypassing strategies and makes us very susceptible to whatever influences legitimize dissociation from the body.

Getting back to the body is a matter not of sliding back into our past but of bringing ourselves into and past our past, unraveling and disarming whatever might seduce us away from the present moment. Getting back to the body involves a relocation and redistribution of attentiveness; this is meta-movement, not movement from here to there, but from here to a deeper here, from now to a deeper now.

Our body says much about our past, including our remote past. The body is shaped by where it has been—and where has it not been? It is elementally continuous with the entire universe: Forms within forms, blooming and withering, evolving and disappearing, birthing and dying, matter and yet not matter, mattering and yet not mattering, every last bit of it contingently bound. We are embodying something particular and at the same time something so enormous and ungraspable that imagination cannot touch it.

And still, our usual self is just a thought away. In just one moment of distracted attention our disconnected self is resurrected, along with our comfortable, everyday sense of familiarity. Instead of using our thinking mind in the service of who we really are, we tend to exploit its attributes, using our reasoning and contextualizing powers to distance ourselves from the very pain and longing that we need to face, separating out from our body-reality as we do so, becoming no-bodies.

When we desensitize ourselves to our body, we tend to associate knowledge and wisdom only with our thinking mind. We try to think our way through life, giving ourselves a break from our minds every now and then by drugging ourselves, having sex, or otherwise using the body as a tool for distraction. Our bodies get so easily saturated with our mental activity—if someone asks us how we're feeling, many of us tend to look up or away, scanning through our mind for the answer. As if the mind knows!

Getting back to the body not only speeds our healing, anchoring and centering us, it also helps decentralize egoity so that we become more than embodied ego and its imperialistic holdings. Getting back to the body isn't about having ego-governed relationships with our different "parts"—part of me wants this, part of me wants that, and another part of me doesn't want either, and so on, revealing not healthy ambiguity but only self-fragmentation—it is about having a being-centered relationship with all that constitutes us.

The body is our medium for being in relationship with our environment (a physical body for a physical environment, a dream body for a dream environment, and so on). But embodiment *is* relationship. As we mature, we shift from sensing our body as a solid something to sensing it as something far from static, something through which we are revealed and expressed, no matter in what state we may be.

When lost in thought, we have no body.

When attention is brought to thought, we have a body.

When attention is brought to sensation, we shift from having a body to being in a body.

When attention is brought to perception, we shift from being in a body to being present as a body.

When attention is brought to our overall presence, our innate wholeness of being, we shift from being present as a body to simply being, neither separate from nor identified with our body.

As we shift from having a body to being a body to simply Being, we find ourselves not just coming home, but sitting at the hearth. In consciously and responsibly embodying all that we are, we become increasingly intimate with all that is. We may still be a relatively solid somebody, but we're now no longer so much in our own way. Spiritual bypassing will have lost its appeal for us. We'll know right to our core that real freedom is not limited by its limitations. Disembodiment will cease to be an option. Doing some time in the chambers of spiritual bypassing was just part of the curriculum on our sojourn to integration. No grades, no Oscars for awakening; we simply repeat our lessons until we have learned them by heart. The body electric, the body speaking its mind, the body-as-spirit, will—if we allow it—blast through our psychoemotional slumber, bringing us into a more integral wholeness until we clearly are in body what we are in spirit.

TRUE RESPONSIBILITY

Heart, Guts, Accountability

Spiritual bypassing can often manifest as a distorted sense of responsibility, in which self-judgment overwhelms a more balanced, open approach to our feelings and behavior. At such times, we confuse responsibility and blame, diminishing ourselves and others in the process and letting a spiritually myopic righteousness possess us, along with minimal concern for whomever we are targeting.

Where taking responsibility expands and strengthens us, blame contracts and weakens us. Taking responsibility empowers us; blame empowers our inner critic. Taking responsibility enhances intimacy; blame inhibits it. When we are busy blaming, we are devoid of compassion, presenting our case in psychoemotional courtrooms as cramped as they are poorly lit. If we are blaming ourselves, we zero in on our questionable behavior, skewering and shrink-wrapping ourselves with guilt, keeping ourselves contracted and in the dark. Whether aimed at others or at ourselves, blame has no heart, regardless of how "spiritually" it may be conveyed. It is easy to pollute ourselves with blame's developmentally arrested morality, in which guilt and condemnation take turns masquerading as conscience. It's not so easy to take real responsibility for our lives.

True responsibility has heart without being mushy or making excuses. For example, if I hurt you, I need to openly and clearly acknowledge that I have done so without self-flagellation, groveling, or other expressions of self-blame (and without denying—or overemphasizing—that other factors that have nothing to do with me may have also contributed to your feeling hurt). Guilting myself for hurting you does not serve you at all and in fact keeps me removed not only from you but also from what I did, as taking that internal beating conveniently distracts me from the situation and potentially lessens your desire to hurt me back.

By contrast, openly expressing remorse for what I did doesn't require that I cringe or shrink or lose my dignity but rather that I use the recognition of my sloppy behavior to help heal and perhaps also deepen whatever connection I already have with you. Responsibility is wide-awake conscience; any shame that it catalyzes simply spurs us into doing whatever we can to bring about healthy resolution.

When we are busy blaming ourselves for our mistakes, we are not really holding ourselves accountable; we are in fact holding ourselves hostage, beating ourselves up before others can do so. This is the essence of guilt, an inherently self-divisive emotion in which one aspect of us, fixatedly childish and irresponsible, triggers our guilt and gets punished shortly thereafter by a fixatedly parental aspect of us. Guilt keeps us small, "safely" tucked away from truly taking charge of our lives. It constitutes a refusal to sanely parent ourselves, relegating us to the domain of blame.

Where blame focuses on put-downs, responsibility seeks to put things right.

Essential for taking responsibility is accountability, or the ability and willingness to acknowledge our role in a particular situation and to accept the consequences of our actions. Those who hold themselves accountable for their words and deeds are reliable, solid, dependable, and trustworthy. They can, in short, be counted on.

There are levels to taking responsibility. At first we may simply own up to what we've done and then do what is minimally necessary to make amends. With practice and increasing awareness, we may later go beyond the call of duty, surrendering to a deeper ethic of accountability, moving from just following the rules that seem to govern any given situation to honoring the spirit of such rules. Taking responsibility is initially a good soldier but at its most mature levels it is a great warrior, alive in many dimensions of conscience.

I recall hearing a story about a woman with a life-threatening illness who believed that she had created the whole thing; she worked very hard to heal it but had no success, which only amplified her sense of herself as defective. Finally she went to a faith healer and was miraculously healed of her illness in a very short time. Shortly thereafter she committed suicide, leaving behind a note in which she said, with great shame, that if it was so easy for her to get healed, and that if she herself could not do this despite having created the whole thing, then she was undeserving to live. This is the dark side of the New Age assertion that we, and we alone, create our illnesses; what debilitating shame and mortification can follow from such a naive belief! This woman believed she was taking responsibility for her illness, but in fact she was just blaming herself for it, losing all compassion for herself in the process.

The notion of taking responsibility is not as simple as it may sound. We might, for example, assume all of the responsibility for what happens between us and our partner, not because we are some sort of nobly altruistic being but simply because we do not want to have to depend on anyone else (probably because in our early years our dependency was badly handled). In assuming responsibility for too much, we are actually being irresponsible, depriving our partner of the experience and growth that come from taking responsibility for what one does. We are, in fact, not being responsible to our relationship but have usurped the *appearance* of responsibility for our own ends, acting from an underlying agenda to avoid painful situations.

Even if we are getting a relatively clear read on what's happening, we may nonetheless still frame our experience in ways that reinforce old habits. For example, if we are dependent on others' approval or are prone to being overly self-critical, we will likely turn our apparent self-reflection into an exercise in self-deception or self-flagellation. And at the same time, we may feel a certain pride in our willingness to take such an unguarded, unflattering look at ourselves when we are in fact doing something very different—namely, submitting to our conditioning while acting as if we are not.

Spiritual bypassing often includes an emphasis on taking responsibility for all that we do, but what is meant by "taking responsibility" in that context is a spiritualized blaming that gives self-reflection a bad name. By focusing too much on what we are doing and believing ourselves to be wholly accountable for any given situation, we pay far too little attention to dynamics other than our own. Self-reflection—an essential ingredient in taking responsibility—is not always what it appears to be. For example, if our conditioning is running the show, there won't be much clarity or depth to our introspection, given the opacity and distortion of the lens. Being overly identified with our conditioning blinds and constricts us, leaving us oblivious to our case of mistaken identity until sufficiently strong forces shake us awake.

This brings us to one of the most overlooked emotions in psychotherapy and spiritual practice: shame. Shame usually feels so unpleasant, so painfully exposing and so mortifying, that we understandably want to get away from it as quickly as possible. A particularly common way of doing so is to convert our shame into anger, and often aggression—just think of how often those who have been shamed redirect their energies into getting even or getting revenge. But anger, which is a more socially acceptable emotion for men than for women, is not always directed outward; it can also be directed inward. Many people (more often male than female) turn their shame-catalyzed anger onto their loved ones, finding fault with, for example, a partner's delivery of what they have to say, thereby conveniently framing them as the messed-up one. Many others (more often female than male) turn their shame-catalyzed anger back onto themselves, casting an overly critical eye on their shortcomings or on how they might have better expressed their position or needs, thereby avoiding an overt display of anger and cutting their partner too much slack.

Just as there is blind compassion, blind humility (making a virtue out of self-effacement to avoid standing out), and blind tolerance (exhibiting an undiscriminating acceptance and force-fed egalitarianism), there is blind responsibility: holding ourselves—or letting ourselves be held—overly accountable, as if doing so is an act of integrity, when in fact all we're really doing is setting ourselves up for self-blame and guilt. (After all, if we've "created" our disease or relational difficulty with our partner and we can't get rid of it, aren't we failing?)

This tendency to take too much of the responsibility for our relational difficulties is rooted in a disempowered sense of self, in which a healthy ego structure is supplanted by an identification with being bad or not good enough. Focusing on our faults reinforces this diminished sense of self, even as we attempt to make up for it by being "good." Yes, what bothers us about our partner may speak volumes about us—what we don't like about him or her may indeed be a projection of what we don't like about ourself—but to assume that whatever bothers us is no more than a reflection of something in us prevents our taking necessary stands with our partner.

When we spiritually legitimize the belief that we each create whatever ills and misfortunes befall us, we dig ourselves into an even more problematic mindset about events over which we have little or no control. If a girl is raped, and we assume she has "created" the situation (as, say, a karmic lesson for herself) and is therefore responsible for it, we are, however inadvertently, justifying the rape, perhaps asking what lessons she was trying to teach herself by having "chosen" to be raped. In the pantheon of dumb questions, this is a top contender, wrapped up in appallingly insensitive and disembodied metaphysics. If someone is abusing us and we choose to view the situation as something we have created, then we are just doing time in a me-centered hell and have turned away from taking a necessary stand.

While it's true that we can have a great impact on our world, this does not mean that we literally cause our reality to be brought into being. Being responsible for our actions is not the same as being solely responsible for creating our reality. This is a tricky area because sometimes we can have such an impact on our environment that we radically alter it, as when the symptoms of a deadly disease miraculously leave us. Since every situation has so many factors at play, so many causes and causes of causes ad infinitum in staggeringly complex interplay, we cannot conclusively say—let alone prove—that we, and we alone, create our reality. If we tell someone who has cancer that they are responsible for their illness because they created it and then ask them what lessons they are trying to teach themselves by making themselves so ill, we are not only ignorant of their situation (there are so many factors involved in having cancer that we cannot possibly account for all of them), we are also trying to implant in them the toxic notion that they must have really screwed up somewhere (beyond obvious factors, such as emotional health and diet) to have gotten cancer, forgetting that many great saints had cancer, regardless of *their* degree of illumination.

Genuine responsibility is the capacity to both recognize our part in whatever is happening and to respond appropriately to it—physically, mentally, emotionally, spiritually, morally—rather than just reacting to or avoiding it. Such responsibility does not engage in shaming or blaming; it does not distract us from confronting others when necessary or fall prey to the inappropriate assuming of agency and authorship (as in "I am responsible for it all"). Instead it stabilizes us, grounding us in the integrity and real compassion that support a deeper, fully embodied life. Through our efforts we enter a domain where self-reflection is no longer self-deflection, and where being responsible is not just something we do but something that we naturally are.

SPIRITUAL GULLIBILITY AND CULTISM

There is such a glut of half-baked spiritual expertise in contemporary culture, such a surfeit of egos wrapped up in spiritual robes, such an abundance of shallowness and delusion masquerading as genuine spirituality, that it has become increasingly difficult to identify truly legitimate, transformative practices. Our instant-gratification society is particularly susceptible to promises of quick-fix self-improvement, and this extends into the spiritual improvement realm, where both cottage- and corporate-sized industries flourish.

Many of us who are otherwise quite rational and capable of critical thinking may find ourselves eager to escape the ongoing pain of our unresolved wounds and unmet needs through methods that promise to deliver us from our suffering as easily and magically as possible. If we are used to doubting ourselves, focusing too much on our own shortcomings and fears, we may find ourselves drawn to spiritual bypassing's more ambitious marketers and entrepreneurs who, exuding self-confidence and fearlessness, seductively market their teachings and supposed metaphysical gifts to the spiritually vulnerable.

If we won't permit ourselves a healthy suspicion when we hear that an "expert" we're skeptical of is claiming to be a healer or dharma teacher, we'll likely suppress our doubts and instead go along with a group's assertion that the person is a true healer or dharma teacher (especially if many in our social circle are doing so). Or we might not raise a discriminating eyebrow after hearing someone's announcement of being enlightened—after all, how do we know their claim isn't true? And on it goes until we retrieve a healthy skepticism so that our spiritual and critical faculties can beneficially coexist.

Because those of us prone to spiritual gullibility tend to confuse skepticism with cynicism, believing that trust in the world is a more ideal spiritual state, we may fail to exercise the necessary discernment in vetting those whose income or self-worth largely depends upon our spiritual gullibility. Our lack of discrimination here has the unfortunate effect of throwing together both the flaky and the genuine elements of contemporary spirituality.

In spiritual gullibility, we tend to confuse love with sentimentality, anger with aggression, compassion with pity, kindness with niceness, intelligence with cleverness, acceptance with exaggerated tolerance, and receptivity with passivity—thus losing ourselves in an openness that lacks healthy boundaries, a "yes" gutted by our inability or unwillingness to say a fully embodied "no" to those to whom we attribute spiritual authority. However, once the spiritually gullible have awakened to their folly, they may go to the other extreme and condemn as charlatans the great majority of those who practice and teach spirituality outside of the mainstream (the wide-eyed devotee and the cynical dismisser of all things New

Age being two sides of the same spiritually blind coin).

Sharp, sophisticated intellects are sometimes found in cults or in other dysfunctional spiritual communities (which still feature plenty of cultic elements) where the leader's authority, however heavy-handed, is rarely questioned, mostly because followers have not yet dealt with their core wounds and conditioning. (And how many cults—and just about every organization has cultic elements—deal in any real depth with transference issues between student and teacher?) People will often give (and give up) anything to be part of something that delivers, or that convincingly promises to deliver, a stable sense of belonging. Like lovers who abandon their boundaries, confusing fusion with intimacy until the rude awakening of their differences begins to dawn, followers of any cult, however benign it may seem, tend to dissolve too much of their identity into group-think without maintaining a robust sense of discerning individuality.

There is such an abundance of spiritual gullibility in our culture that those who are drawn to take advantage of it will, more often than not, soon have a following or at least a clientele that unquestioningly buys what is being sold—which tends to reinforce beliefs that they are someone very special, with great untapped powers to be realized. The commodification of spirituality, with all its promises of a more spiritual you in an appealingly short time, has understandably attracted intense entrepreneurial interest. Those who market themselves to the spiritually gullible are not, for the most part, con artists, since they usually believe in themselves and what they are doing—they may even view their most blatant manipulations as no more than necessary steps in helping others heal. Just as unresolved wounds lead some people to seek quick fixes and to follow a powerful figure, other people deflect these wounds by making themselves into such a powerful figure that their wounds appear to be nonexistent, and they may further reinforce this apparent immunity by encouraging a following that is more cult than community.

I don't mean "cult" here in the automatically pejorative, sensationalistic sense but rather in the sense of a self-enclosed entity that is both overattached to its core beliefs and almost impermeable to outside feedback and internal dissension. Cults can be relatively benign; they also can be exceedingly destructive (as Jonestown or Nazism were). The range of cultic behavior is enormous: ego can arguably be seen as a cult of one; plenty of couples function as cults of two; and various religious and political movements are cults of the many.

Cultism overseparates: It is a tightly encapsulated, self-obsessed *us,* with the rest of existence becoming a rather distant *them.* Whatever caring exists within cultism—and it can be a very deep, however misguided, caring—is eventually impoverished by its isolation from the rest of life. At best, cults protect what is inside their walls, but sooner or later they become guards rather than guardians. If the alienation, painful sense of separateness, or estrangement that so often drives us to seek membership with a group is not properly addressed so that our yearning for togetherness is not just an escape from our sense of alienation, we'll remain highly susceptible to the pull of various parental or "we have the answer" institutions and movements.

It is easy to become overly attached to any person or group that appears to provide for us. However, in becoming part of a group mentality we enter into an allegiance that actually reinforces the very separateness that first propelled us toward our particular support system. But what exactly is it that is being supported? Does the hand that feeds us expect us to convert to its faith or guidelines? Are we more likely to keep getting fed if we do? Is there an ulterior motive, and, if so, do we see it, or do we even *want* to see it? How many organizations (including spiritual communities) include—or even want to include—within themselves a self-investigative branch, one that has unimpeded access to resources outside the organization (including people who might bring the kind of criticism that could necessitate its dismantling or radical reorganization)?

What happens when the shelter that once gave us so much needed support becomes too tight or poor a fit? Do we then believe ourselves to be in the wrong, assuming that we must be doing something to generate our sense of restlessness or being stifled, or do we instead challenge the very structure and foundational assumptions of such a shelter, no matter how convincingly our protests might be labelled "resistance," "our problem," or mere adolescent reactivity? Even the most supportive of groups can easily become confining webs, entangling us in their expectations and morality. Thus do cults arise, populated to a large degree by those who are spiritually gullible.

Spiritual gullibility is big business in our consumer-driven economy. We want it fast—whatever "it" is. Those who want our business know this well and advertise accordingly, counting on our credulity (which typically gets framed as openness or receptivity). Their promises are often so outrageous (as exemplified by the "you can manifest whatever you want" selling points of positive-thinking purveyors) that our unquestioned, even enthusiastic reception speaks of deep naiveté infused with an understandable longing to have a better tomorrow with as little fuss or pain as possible.

Spiritual gullibility constitutes not just a too-naive openness but also a regression, a dropping back into the prerational, magical thinking mode of childhood. This leaves us not childlike but childish, opening not only our hearts and minds but also our wallets indiscriminately, all the while thinking that we are getting the real deal. The antidote, however, is not to become suspicious of or averse to spirituality and metaphysics but rather to develop a keen sense of discernment that does not restrict our capacity to open to the world, making us capable of cult-transcending relationship and community, able to give ourselves fully without giving ourselves away.

Spiritual gullibility's slumbering innocence, when met with a discerning eye and perhaps also a fitting dose of fierce compassion, transforms into a wakeful, ever-fresh, and unexploitable openness that realigns us with What Really Matters.

ARE WE RESPONSIBLE FOR OUR ILLNESS?

Are we responsible for our illness? There is plenty packed into this question and so the answer requires more than just a simplistic "yes" or "no." There are many people who believe that we are responsible—fully responsible—for our illnesses, regardless of other contributing factors. Not surprisingly, many of those who adhere to such a belief are firm believers in the notion that we create our own reality, particularly through our thoughts. For them, illness is considered the result of a kind of thought disorder, with negative thinking being the primary culprit. The exaggerated optimism of this kind of belief in positive thinking tends to run roughshod over any dissenting (read "negative") opinions.

While the concept of positive thinking pre-dates the New Age movement, it has been increasingly usurped by and abused in spiritual bypassing circles to the point that a judgmental, uncompassionate "pick yourself up by your own bootstraps" mentality has become widespread and is applied to one and all, including those with terminal illnesses. The idea that we create our own reality and can control every aspect of our lives if only we will it strongly enough has become popularized through much of New Age spirituality, especially through the prosperity consciousness gospel and the laws of attraction peddled in books like *The Secret.* The shadow elements of these sunnyside-up, "you-can-have-it-all" concepts should not be underestimated. They have spawned such beliefs as the notion that we are completely responsible for our illness or for anything else that happens to us simply because we, and we alone, have created it. Thus it is our fault if we have cancer or any other disease; to hold anything else responsible, from environmental factors to genetics, is simply delusion. If we really want to be well, and totally believe that we will get well, then we will of course get well; and if we don't get well, it must be because we didn't really want to get well. After all, we create our reality, don't we? If we are sick, it must be because we have chosen it for ourselves.

Those who adhere to such a belief system leave themselves very little room in which to maneuver when they find out that they have a serious illness—they believe that they have brought it into being, that they and they alone are responsible for it. This generates powerful conditions for the arising of guilt—if I now have cancer, then I must have done something wrong; otherwise, I wouldn't have cancer. Adherence to this New Age dogma means that rather than fully exploring the nature of our illness, we may be further debilitated by guilt for having supposedly created something as life-negating and unspiritual as cancer.

The belief that we literally create our reality often carries a certain grandiosity, uncritically attributing inordinate or impossible power to our capacity for wishing and wanting and imagining, as described in the magical thinking chapter. Such me-centered overestimations of personal power are quite natural to young children, but not to adults. Those spiritual practitioners who are caught up in this belief, perhaps influenced by what they have heard from high-profile teachers of New Age spirituality, may feel inflated by the idea that they alone create their reality but inevitably must become flattened by it, given how far short of their goals they will find themselves. Unfortunately, falling short of one's goals is rarely used as an opportunity to critically examine these beliefs about reality-creation but instead becomes an occasion to shame oneself for having "failed."

While it may be true that in some cases our behavior has made the onset of a disease more likely, this does not, however, mean that we actually *caused* our illness; rather that there appears to be a positive correlation between some of our actions or choices and the presence of our illness. If I am eating a diet loaded with sugar, unhealthy fats, and hormone-suffused red meat, and I am highly stressed, sedentary, and sleep-deprived, then I am increasing the odds that I will get cancer, heart disease, or diabetes. The fact that some people who have very healthy diets and lifestyles still get ill does not invalidate this point. There are so many factors involved in the arising of a particular disease—including factors over which we have no control—that we cannot decisively say which one actually caused the disease.

Conversely, some people say that we are not at all responsible for whatever disease we have. Proponents of this view see an illness like cancer as an alien invasion that can strike anyone, regardless of how healthy or young that person is. These people point to our increasingly carcinogenic environment as an inescapable reality, which can only be partially combated by healthy practices. They also point to the emergence of cancer in young children to show that cancer is not something for which we are responsible. After all, who would blame a young child for his or her cancer? But by focusing solely on the external or purely biological factors of cancer, they go too far in the other direction, discounting any contributing psychological and emotional factors in their view of why we get sick.

If, after learning that we have a major illness, we see things we may have done that contributed to our getting sick, we do not have to blame ourselves for our choices but can instead compassionately recognize how those choices arose and affected us, and from this realization bring ourselves into a deeper sense of wholeness. No guilt—just a deeper opening to and understanding of our situation. It's important to realize that by chronically beating ourselves up we miss out on developing a profound relationship to our illness—and to ourselves. Many people have reported that having a serious illness was the best thing that ever happened to them, as it forced a long-overdue change of priorities and a richer appreciation of life.

Once we recognize how some of our choices may have contributed to our getting ill, we can begin to work with them, exploring their origins and anatomy, making room for more life-giving choices to emerge. For example, I can look back and see how driven I have been, for better or for worse, since I was in high school; yes, I also learned to meditate deeply, to really relax, but I still kept driving myself on in most areas of my life. Did this create my prostate cancer (with which I was diagnosed in October 2008)? No. Did it create conditions conducive to the arising of my cancer? Probably. And does ceasing to drive myself so hard, which I am now doing, mean that my cancer will disappear? Not necessarily. But letting that drivenness soften and ease, level upon level, makes me more receptive to what I truly need, leaving me more dynamically alive, more open to both my death and my life, all of which I strongly intuit is increasing the odds of healing (or at least radically reducing) my cancer. Will the odds be increased enough? I don't know. It's enough that I am alive and becoming more alive.

If we don't heal from our illness, despite doing all we can to deal with it, this is not a sign of failure! All we can do is work as best we can with the factors over which we have some influence. It is simply magical thinking to assume that if we just wish or affirm or visualize it hard enough, we can overcome our illness. Yes, bringing a spacious awareness to our condition, in conjunction with a wholehearted faith in our body's capacity to heal itself, can certainly help, but it may not be enough. It is profoundly humbling—and profoundly practical—to simply sit with what we cannot control.

I did not create my cancer, but I am responsible for many of the factors that made its arising possible—not guilty, but responsible. I am not at war with my cancer, but I am in deep dialogue with it. As I listen to my cancer, I hear more than my cancer—and am immeasurably deepened and awakened through doing so. It is my sobering joy to be as responsible as I can to my cancer, to do all I can to cease feeding it so that it does not obstruct my living. Rather than attacking it, I am cutting off its supply lines as much as possible, with some very skilled help. Will this save me? I don't know, but I'm not doing it only to save myself but to deepen my life. I would love to live much longer for all kinds of reasons—and I feel strongly aligned with whatever might bring that about—but I know that my time may be much shorter than I would like. Being at ease with this is not at all fatalistic but rather realistic, bringing me into deepening intimacy both with what dies and with what does not die.

WHEN NONDUAL TEACHINGS ARE NOT NONDUAL

At their best, nondual teachings are lucid reminders of what we truly are, demonstrating that the inherent inseparability of all that exists is neither a concept nor an experience nor something to attain but our very nature. The reality of all-pervading nonseparation (variously called One Taste or God or Suchness or Natural Great Perfection) is ever present, shining through all the entrapping dreams we habitually fuel and occupy.

We may conceive of nonduality as a place, a stage, or an achievement; but it is simply what we already are, both transcending and simultaneously including everything. Caught up in our usual activities, having forgotten our true nature, we may seem to be elsewhere, but we are in fact never truly apart from it. This radical truth is not something to merely believe in—as happens in spiritual bypassing—but to live and to fully embody.

In nonduality there is no dissociation from phenomena, no withdrawal from life, no bypassing, no avoidance of manifesting as form. And there is no truly separate self, no discrete knower, no autonomous entity standing apart from and seeing all of this. There is no past, no future, and nowhere to go, just a freedom beyond imagining. This may sound like madness to our usual self but not to who we really are. To our mind, nonduality is inescapably and unyieldingly paradoxical, but to our heart of hearts, it is living truth. In nondual awareness the personality is no longer the locus of self but nonetheless still persists—and why shouldn't it? If we are truly at home in (and *as*) the nondual, then personality, like everything else, is just one more nonbinding expression of nondual being, needing not annihilation but rather recognition and acceptance (and this is precisely where spiritual bypassing gets really hung up, as we shall see). To nondual awareness, everything is God—anger, joy, duality, personality, clouds, wonder, fear. There is only the Real, only the One, only the Mystery, outshining any language with which we attempt to describe it—and if we genuinely recognize this, there is no abandonment of our humanness, no employing of nondual teachings to separate out from the more difficult challenges of life, no turning away from the demands of relationship.

From a truly nondual perspective, if fear or any other apparently undesirable state arises, there is no problem whatsoever. In the nondual, it is not our fear that is transcended but what we do with fear in dualistic states.

These teachings, however, can easily be misunderstood and twisted into the service of spiritual bypassing's agendas. Perspectives that are conceptually rooted rather than truly grounded in the nondual are particularly problematic. Behind the equanimity-infused half-smiles that are perhaps ever so gently flickering across the faces of those teachers of the nondual who are caught up in spiritual bypassing, something very personal, something decidedly not nondual, may be seeking expression, which of course cannot be permitted, as the attachments, anger, or egoity of the teacher might be revealed.

It is easy to use nondual teachings to both distance ourselves from our humanity and to make a virtue of such disengagement, leaving us clinging to our detachment. We may think we are following these teachings even as we have eviscerated them, stranding ourselves in superficiality. Such distortions are reinforced by teachers who reduce nonduality to a rationale for bypassing our individuality and the "stories" through which we reinforce our sense of self. The spooning out of nondual pablum—prechewed for us—assumes that we have no teeth, no bite, no need for uncooked truth, and should instead just keep our spiritual bibs on.

Where has the wildness, the rawness, the full-blooded embodiment of spirituality gone? Must it be caged, drugged, homogenized, reduced to a squeaky-clean idealism for hungry seekers? Must we play vigilant zookeeper or valium supplier to spirituality's edginess? Must we depersonalize and dehumanize it?

We may, in the throes of embracing nondual philosophy, get so attached to the notion that form is illusion that we shy away from living a relational, fully embodied life, doing time in the sanctums of spiritual correctness. To the extent that form *is* illusion, so are we (at least as we "normally" take ourselves to be)—but in the meantime we have a lot of living and learning and developing to do. To say "it's all an illusion" is a copout, littered with the debris of secondhand understanding and premature claims to advanced spiritual realization; what needs to be recognized is the illusory aspect of whatever is before us, which requires far more than a parroting of the notion that our world is all just an illusion. There is no substitute for firsthand learning.

In order to see through the apparent reality of form—fully experiencing, not just conceptualizing, its essential emptiness—we need to become genuinely intimate with this world of form, resisting the temptation to bypass or marginalize such an undertaking.

Making intellectual real estate out of nondual pronouncements does not constitute wisdom! Better to get out of our heads and start really living and loving *now* instead of going on and on about unconditional love, enlightenment, and other such ideals; better to fully manifest and deeply live our uniqueness instead of going on and on about our inherent inseparability and oneness. Why let the recognition of our innate unity of Being separate us from our differences?

It is very easy to intellectually appropriate nondual teachings and then use them to justify or rationalize some of our actions, such as disrespecting our or others' boundaries. What a treacherously slippery slope this is, laden with mindfields, spiritual naiveté, and the detritus of regurgitated nondual teachings! Truly recognizing the nondual nature of Reality leaves us not immune to the necessities of the everyday dualistic world but even more sensitive and attuned to them, even more capable of sanely and skillfully responding to them, and even more intimate with all that arises.

Spiritual bypassing's approach to nonduality falls into the same trap as does much of postmodern art study, which tends to be more about the over-intellectualization of art than about art itself. Many of those claiming to teach nondual spirituality may cover their tracks with nondual wordplay, but no matter how impressive such lingo may sound, their separation from and refusal to truly embody the dual, the personal, the idiosyncratic, the shadowy, and, yes, the unrepentantly egoic keeps them (and their followers) up to their eyeballs in good old dualism, clinging to the idea—or ideal—of nonduality.

Claims of abiding in nondual awareness run rampant in modern spiritual circles—and how could they not, given that we are deeply embedded in a culture slavishly devoted to quick fixes and highs, spiritual or otherwise? When we try to make too much out of a moment of awakening, we're just creating and reinforcing more of the very selfhood we are so eager to transcend.

Hearing teachings that tell us we already are fully realized, nondual beings who have simply forgotten our true nature may reassure or console us, but in most cases it tends to distract from the work we truly need to do, which includes facing and working with our fear, aggression, greed, shame, and whatever else we've misused or turned away from in ourselves. The central shadow of pseudo-nondualistic teachings is unacknowledged dualism, which is most commonly characterized by a resolute aversion to acknowledging our need to do any in-depth psychological work.

An almost-universally acknowledged sage of the nondual, Ramana Maharshi spoke and acted from a nondual perspective simply because he could not do otherwise. Just as importantly, he wasn't looking for immunity from the raw stuff of life, and he sure wasn't busy being clever with language or theory. He was, in fact, radically available. It is by really living—getting right into the messy stuff of life, including that awakening realm and unparalleled exposer of neuroses and avoidance known as intimate relationship—that we learn the radical integrity and wholeness so essential to a proper understanding of our nondual nature.

While nondual teachings point out the futility of searching for what was never really lost, these teachings often fail to stress that such a search usually is not experienced as futile until it has been undertaken. Thus many spiritual seekers who believe in such teachings get stranded in a no-man's-land, supposedly "above" the developmental levels that they think they have transcended (but in fact have only intellectually skipped). This is what the great Buddhist teacher Nagarjuna meant when he mentioned the trap of *believing* in emptiness. So we might as well jump in, getting messy, getting attached, getting hurt, getting involved, fully participating. We are making an appearance here as humans, so let's really get into it! Only when we're truly involved can we realize with our totality our relationship to All That Is.

Those espousing unskillfully transmitted nondual teachings might say that there is nothing to do because there is no one to do it, thereby creating a philosophical dead-end masquerading as spiritual wisdom. However, the non-doing of the true sage is a far different expression than the non-doing of the rest of us whose understanding remains netted by dualism.

I end this chapter with a deep bow to the true teachers of the nondual, in whose continued presence and love my words stretch beyond themselves, and in whose wisdom my arrogance evaporates, leaving nothing but What Really Matters, whatever form it might take.

BRINGING SHAME OUT OF THE SHADOWS

Probably the most neglected emotion in psychotherapy and spiritual practice is shame, even though it is often the primary emotional force animating our aggression and spiritual ambition. Attitudes toward shame in the spiritual bypassing realm mirror those of secular culture: For most of us, shame is a kind of hell, a deeply branded, insidiously compelling sense of being defective. It is probably the emotion for which we have the most aversion. In a famous poll that asked what people were most afraid of, dying came in third or fourth, while making a fool of oneself when speaking before a crowd topped the list. The fear of making a fool of oneself, the fear of being humiliated, of feeling all-out shame—dogs us both consciously and unconsciously. Fear of such exposure even haunts our sleep, in all those dreams of being suddenly naked at important events, one's clothing nowhere in sight.

And yet, as much as we try to avoid shame, we may well perpetuate shaming behaviors, knowingly or unknowingly. If I am openly showing anger or being critical and you are enmeshed in spiritual bypassing, you are probably going to shame me, however indirectly or subtly, for falling short. You will find me guilty of such actions without taking any responsibility for your own judgments.

Those of us enmeshed in spiritual bypassing won't admit that we shame anyone—we are too loving, too accepting, too damned nice to do such a thing!—but we nonetheless go ahead anyway, couching our criticism in comments such as "I am doing this out of my compassion for you; I offer this feedback freely to do with as you will." These potentially noble words are marred by our underlying agenda. Even when we are caught blatantly shaming others, we usually won't admit it; at most we may say things like "I apologize if my words came across as uncaring or insensitive" or "I take responsibility for tripping over my tongue" or "I'm still learning to say things more clearly." We tend to remain in denial that we're shaming those who fall short of our standards, whether physically, emotionally, mentally, spiritually, or socially. Such alibis masquerade as confessions in an act of spiritual sidestepping.

Shame has the power to instantly change our experience; what a moment ago had been enjoyable can become awkward and disorienting, depriving us of our usual ability to take care of ourselves or ask for a time-out from a potentially difficult situation with others. In the case of healthy shame, we are not put down, however strongly our behaviors are brought under a critical eye, but when shame is unhealthy, we are not so much sobered as crushed and devalued. In its most toxic forms, shame simply grinds us down, making us feel like disappearing or even killing ourselves—hence *mortification.*

Nonetheless, without the capacity for shame, we would be devoid of conscience. In healthy shame, our conscience is clearly and empoweringly activated so that we can make necessary amends, whereas in unhealthy shame our conscience is supplanted by a ruthlessly relentless inner critic, before which we shrink into disempowered states. Instead of continuing to constrict us, healthy shame eventually unknots and opens us; we are enriched with an uncomfortable yet ultimately enlivening passion through our consciously felt responsibility and remorse for what has happened. There is a powerful and deep-rooted impetus for coming clean, letting go, and healing—a painful yet heartfelt resolution to grow.

Healthy shame provides fertile conditions for reconnecting with the parental authority native to us. For example, if we have just put down our partner for not being more spiritually aware, through our openly felt shame over having done so we can take full responsibility for what we've done and also work through whatever drove us to behave in such a hurtful way in the first place. Such shame can catalyze an environment in which genuine forgiveness can bloom, providing an opportunity to come clean and discover a truer way of relating. Unhealthy shame, however, works against the possibility of forgiveness, making us feel so dysfunctional—so inept or dumb or immature or out of touch—that we become disempowered and can very easily be shamed by others, including in spiritual contexts where we are so busy beating ourselves up that we'll go along with practices that aren't good for us.

It's usually not very difficult to shame others. All we have to do is get their inner critic (that heartlessly judgmental internalized voice that many of us tend to question no more than young children would question their parents' authority) all riled up, to zero in on what they already consider to be defective or ugly in themselves, or bring up a failure of theirs that still eats at them. Why would we do such a thing, consciously or unconsciously? Because in shaming others, we bring the heat to them and remove or project it away from ourselves, thereby keeping our cool, whether in secular or spiritual contexts. When we are in the grip of spiritual bypassing and shame those who fall short of our standards, we are likely to argue that we are not shaming them and that if they feel shamed by what we've shared with them, that is just their issue, their lack of love for themselves, and so on.

If we get others squirming with shame, they are probably going to be so busy managing or trying to escape from it that they will have little or no energy to focus on our shortcomings or mistakes. We have successfully made the situation all about them, diverting our responsibility while playing the compassionately impartial observer who speaks only for their highest good. (I'm not talking here about the kind of shame that we ought to feel under certain conditions, but rather about the kind that cripples us, when we lie crushed beneath the boots of our inner critic.)

When we feel shame, we usually quickly—and quite automatically—convert it into or overlay it with other states or feelings like aggression (whether toward others or toward ourselves), withdrawal, avoidance, and dissociation. So, for example, while it might appear in a particular situation that we are dealing with aggression, and aggression only, in fact it is only a *secondary* arising, obscuring the shame that gave rise to it. If we don't know our own shame well, including all the ways in which it can mutate into other feelings and states, we won't be of much use to others who are having difficulty getting close to their own shame.

Though shame itself is not fear, we fear it. We may blend shame with fear, thereby whipping up guilt, or we may push it into the background, letting other emotions take center stage, but in any case, we are avoiding our shame instead of simply acknowledging its presence and sitting with it to the point of cultivating some intimacy with it. The better we know our shame, the better use we will make of it.

Getting close to shame is far from an easy task, however, given how easily it can plunge us into a gripping, darkly burning sense of being seriously flawed in the eyes of a critical audience. No wonder we want to get away from it as quickly as we can! Yet there is such healing and such a deepening of integrity in staying with our shame and mining its gifts. Unlike fear and anger, which ready us for action, shame interrupts us, creating a kind of psychoemotional contraction and collapse that is strong enough to stop us in our tracks. The commonplace slang for psychiatrists, "shrinks," may have its origin in the shame—and accompanying self-shrinkage—that so many have felt when going for psychiatric help, since most patients are put under a diagnostic lens that frames them as defective in some way. Given the power of shame to contract us, it's no surprise that if we espouse expansive spiritual ideals we will have an extremely strong aversion to feeling shame and seek a comforting distance from it through shaming others—which of course we would deny doing.

Of course, not all of us who feel shame engage in shaming behaviors; most of us have developed an endless array of strategies for dodging our feelings. The more defective we take ourselves to be, the more driven we will be to seek some sort of compensatory solution, be it narcissistic behavior, aggression, people pleasing, withdrawal, depression, dissociation, or excessive interest in sex. So much of what we do is just a strategy to avoid shame. So much shame about shame!

In our avoidance of shame we fail to realize the crucial function it serves. For without the capacity for shame, there would be no conscience. The moral hub of shame—and I speak here of healthy shame—is responsibility. On the other hand, the moral hub of guilt—unhealthy shame, or shame polluted with fear—is blame. Guilt frequently masquerades as conscience (as does our inner critic/superego) but healthy shame awakens, or reawakens, conscience. Conscience can be defined as our innate moral sense actively responding to the world, cultivated through a mix of empathy and shame-informed—but not shame-dominated!—contemplation.

Guilt has the capacity to keep us small, stuck, and divided. The childish part of us grabs for the candy while the authoritarian part wields a parental whip, beating us for our transgression (and thereby giving us tacit permission to once again do the "bad" deed, as long as we accept our punishment). Where shame exposes us, guilt splits us. Guilt is not only a refusal to love; it is also a refusal to properly parent ourselves. At its core is a stalemated parent-child relationship, stunting our growth. In our guilt, we childishly cling to—and also react to—outside parental forces that we have internalized. By contrast, healthy shame provides fertile conditions for reconnecting with our native parental authority, propelling us into taking needed responsibility even as we take good care of whatever is childish in us. Guilt mires us; healthy shame frees us.

Shame is usually painfully imbued with self-consciousness—which is a misnomer, since when we are "self-conscious" we are not so much conscious of our self as we are concerned with others watching (or apparently watching) us. Becoming conscious of our self-consciousness—that is, allowing it to be the object rather than the subject of our attention when we are in shame's grip—allows us to examine our shame with at least some degree of healthy detachment.

Better yet, let us bring our shame into our heart, letting its energies branch through us, granting its message, however dark or misshapen, an audience in chambers of compassionate clarity. Of course, this isn't going to work if we won't admit to having shame. If we are caught in spiritual bypassing, there is no way we are going to make such an admission, for to do so would be to lose our sense of identity as spiritual adepts—or at least our cherished illusion of being further along the spiritual path than we actually are. Much as we try to keep our shame safely tucked away from illumination, however, it still leaks out, in our thoughts, words, and actions.

Shame that is not acknowledged, openly felt, shared, and worked with will pollute any relationships in which it arises. So it is essential that we come to know our history with shame inside and out and be able to recognize it as it arises. We have all felt (and very likely still carry some) shame; our work is not to make a problem out of our shame—neither fleeing it nor letting it cripple us—but to instead openly face and work with it.

When first realizing the role that shame has played in our lives, many of us are astonished at how pervasive, deep-cutting, and influential that role has been; it is as if we have discovered a lost continent of ourselves, initially submerged or deeply shrouded in fog, and then illuminated by the spirit of exploration brought to it. Bringing shame out of the shadows is a deeply healing undertaking, a journey that we must take, sooner or later, if we are to truly live. Initially, we probably will not have much awareness of the impact that shame has had— and is having—in our lives. We may, for example, be driven to excel or stand out in a particular way in order to get as far away as possible from failures we suffered long ago, failures for which we were put down, belittled, or otherwise shamed. Our pride in what we can now do is little more than diverted shame, inflating us where we once were deflated. Here, we are highly prone not only to being shamed but also to shaming others. This can be loud and aggressive, and it can also be much more subtle—conveyed, for example, through a quick, barely perceptible rolling of the eyes or through smiling certainties laced ever-so-lightly with rarefied arrogance.

Eventually we reach the point where we rarely shame others because we clearly recognize and feel the consequences of doing so. Then there is no investment in putting down others, no drive to dominate or stand above them. At this stage, we are not strangers to shame's anatomy and workings; we know it well and understand the difference between healthy and unhealthy shame. We no longer let our shame mutate into aggression or relational disengagement. When we feel shame, we openly and quickly admit it. When we slip, we hold ourselves accountable but don't beat ourselves up for our slippage—that is, we don't allow our shame to turn into guilt.

None of this means that shame ceases to exist, but that it has significantly shed its unhealthy forms.

We have, among other things, outgrown our tendency for spiritual bypassing. Getting away from what troubles us has become less interesting than going toward it.

Do not underestimate how subtle shame can get. Let's consider this in the context of a common kind of shaming: the questioning of competence. Imagine that our competence in an area in which we are highly skilled is called into question by significant others. Despite no evidence of incompetence on our part, we are being shamed, however obliquely or slightly, and we can feel it. We may then accuse ourselves of being oversensitive or of just imagining that we are being put down, especially if we look up to the people questioning our competence and they assure us that they are not putting us down.

Shame can get in through the tiniest cracks. Once in, it can spread with poisonous ease throughout us. We can be shamed not just for falling short but also for not admitting that we may have fallen short (even when we clearly have not fallen short). We can be shamed for not showing shame. We can be shamed for simply being alive. We can be shamed for taking things personally. We can be shamed for feeling deeply. When we allow ourselves to be shamed, we feel disempowered and are left too vulnerable to what our shamers are telling us.

Here again, the inner critic that plagues many of us may masquerade as a messenger of healthy criticism, but it is actually just a loveless loudmouth, the relentless voice of self-deprecation in morality's robes. When we look at ourselves or others through the eyes of our inner critic, all we see are flaws and imperfections; things to be corrected. It's crucial to remember that healthy criticism does not shame, it does not condescend, and it does not belittle. A mature spiritual practice demands that we actively engage our faculties of discernment, all the while remaining vigilant of our inner critic's judgmental tendencies. As we learn to relate to our inner critic instead of from it, we vastly reduce the power it has over us. Then we can, with full authority, say to our inner critic: "You are *not* me!" and see through its shaming tactics.

As we mature, we drop our defenses against shame, accessing the courage to stand in its painful fire without letting it shapeshift into aggression or disconnection. By deepening our intimacy not just with our shame but also with our escapist tendencies, we come to realize that real freedom is not about getting away from what is troubling us but rather about going into and through it. We may emerge with a few scars and probably a little less skin, but emerge we do, no longer bypassing our less flattering qualities. This is fierce, unconditioned love for ourselves, alive with a spiritual boldness that serves us all.

WHEN OUR HONEYMOON WITH SPIRITUALITY IS OVER

When our honeymoon with spirituality ends—when our desire to be spiritually correct and fashionable fades, and spiritual bypassing no longer holds any significant appeal for us—we may retreat into disillusionment for a while. This may not feel very good, but it is necessary, as it will clear our vision so that spirituality can be deglamorized and divested of its less-than-spiritual motives and payoffs. Life after spiritual bypassing and spiritual correctness is the beginning of authentic spirituality. No fireworks, no applause, no need to advertise ourselves as someone spiritual. No grandiosity, no fake humility. That which is supposedly unspiritual will no longer automatically be shunned or bypassed. The longing to be fully awakened will still be present but without the desperation and ambition that once characterized it. Where once we were in a hurry to achieve an idealized goal, we are no longer rushing or pushing, having resolved that we are in it for the long haul, that the journey is the teacher.

What are we to do with spiritual bypassing? First of all, learn to recognize it and name it. Keep it far enough away to keep it in focus and close enough to feel its contours. Over time, our increasing familiarity with the inner dynamics of spiritual bypassing helps us understand what we have been avoiding and why. As this wisdom grows, we no longer split ourselves into antagonistic factions. Instead of being at war with our weaknesses, we bring them into our heart. Instead of trying to get rid of what we don't like about ourselves, we develop a better relationship to all that we are. Thus intimacy rather than transcendence becomes our path.

Most of the books will be gone; the ones that remain will feel like old friends that we don't tire of revisiting, even if only for a page or two every month or so. Many of the practices will also be gone; the ones that remain usually will feel as natural to slip into as our favorite jeans or T-shirt, at ease both with being worn and being worn out. Most of our aspirations to be spiritual will also be gone; the ones that remain will feel like unforced breaths, okay in the beginning, okay in the middle, and okay at the end.

Our guilt over doing "unspiritual" things will be replaced by a benevolently firm oversight that brings to them a spacious, understanding perspective. If some issues remain in the shadows, we approach rather than flee them, armed not with rehabilitation flyers and spiritual slogans but with a compassion at once tender and fierce. And whatever disciplines we take on will result not from one aspect of us dominating the rest but from a core recognition of what is needed, as the different aspects of ourselves function with an underlying unity and we allow our choices to emerge from this innate sense of wholeness.

Conscious alignment with the Real becomes not our goal but our ground.

Our focus on what might be will yield to a focus on the here-and-now as hope for the future is replaced by lucid faith, a radical trust in life and its inherent ever-unfolding mystery. Our egoity will not be in the way nearly as much as when we were caught up in spiritual bypassing, and we won't mind our ego's acting out any more than we mind anything else that provides scenery and drama along the journey. We no more want to eradicate ego than does the sky want to eradicate its dark clouds. There is work to be done, and we already have our shoulder to the wheel; our steps may be small, but we are taking them and are grateful that we can do so. No matter how much knowledge we have, we keep opening to the Mystery, allowing revelation to be more central than heady explanation. And as we become more and more open spiritually, our individuality deepens and blooms.

Such movement, such spiritual deepening, marks the beginning of freedom from the conventional self and its programs. Our sense of self shifts from me-centered to we-centered to being-centered, without any dissociation from feeling, for the more being-centered we become, the more embodied and clearly individualized we are. True individuality dynamically coexists with everything that constitutes us, including our spiritual dimensions; through it we both flesh out our essential uniqueness to the fullest and keep ourselves transparent to that which transcends all individuality. In spiritual bypassing we confuse surface with depth. There is no such confusion once we have outgrown spiritual bypassing. Whether we ascend or descend, contract or expand, go inward or outward, we do not lose touch with our core of being for very long. As we start allowing everything—everything!—to awaken us to who and what we truly are, it becomes increasingly clear that while our sense of self comes and goes, *we* don't.

Even though we may outgrow spiritual bypassing, it is important to remember that almost all of us have lapsed into it at times and that the tendency to do so exists in everyone. We might even say that spiritual bypassing is an anti-spiritual practice, since it distances and disconnects us from the very conditions we need to face to embody our true nature. Our work is to not bypass spiritual bypassing; we must give the fear and distress that help catalyze it room enough to both be themselves and to outgrow their agendas, so that their energies can be used for more life-giving purposes.

Life after spiritual bypassing is a committed apprenticeship to What Really Matters. Every situation is part of the curriculum and practicum, offering the same fundamental opportunity to deepen our awakening, especially when we release our experience from any obligation to make us feel better or more secure. In so doing we can still the mind and ground the body, breaking open to what we were born to do and be.

Spiritual bypassing is worth outgrowing. All we have to do is stop turning away from our pain and consciously enter it. This means an end to disembodied living, an end to spiritualized dissociation, an end to emotional illiteracy and relational immaturity. As we commit ourselves to a full-blooded awakening rooted in the cultivation of intimacy with all that we are, we find a willingness to bring whatever we have kept in the dark out into the open. And from this newfound openness we emerge with the gifts of our hard work: firsthand wisdom that benefits one and all.

Authentic spiritual life is the opportunity of a lifetime. It is a constant dying into a deeper life. Emerging from our own ashes becomes no big deal; it's just the way things are. Here the ten thousand sorrows and the ten thousand joys intermingle in unparalleled song, we their infinite notes and the music that goes on, in the one moment that is all moments.

THE METHOD OF NO METHOD

Intuitive Integral Psychotherapy

Note: *Although what follows is written primarily to those who are practicing psychotherapists, it is intended for anyone who is in psychotherapy, who is considering doing some psychotherapy, or who is interested in what psychotherapy can be, especially in the context of spiritual practice.*

To truly consider any psychotherapeutic method or practice is also to consider what we as psychotherapists are doing with it—and not just with regard to our clients. To what degree do we operate from behind our method or rely too much on it, fitting our clients to a particular model rather than fitting it to our clients? To what degree are we trapped or stagnating in our method or rationalizing such entrapment or stagnation? Are we employing it, or is it employing us?

If we were to sit before our clients with no method in mind and no investment in any particular method, what might happen? When we don't know what to do with a client, what do we then do? Do we hunker down behind some set methodology or do we become more dynamically receptive? Questions like these need not be mental mosquitoes ricocheting around inside our heads; instead they can serve as a potent entry into deeper considerations of therapeutic methodology and our degree of investment in them.

As an example, let's briefly examine the practice of giving clients incomplete sentences to finish, with a special emphasis on the inherent directiveness of such a practice—a no-no in therapeutic circles that say not to direct a client. Yes, having clients finish incomplete sentences that I give them is directive, but in this I am, as much as possible, allowing their response (which is encouraged to be spontaneous) to direct me to what comes next, be it to give them another incomplete sentence to finish (catalyzed by my attunement to them and their history, along with my intuitive response to what they have just said and how they said it), to have them describe in some detail what they are now experiencing, to bring more awareness to their breath, to begin some bodywork, or to guide them into some emotional or meditative deepening.

In this, whatever form it may take, my task is not simply to operate from behind a set methodology but to respond as freshly, creatively, caringly, and as effectively as possible, being ready to shift course at any time (which means I have to be willing and able to drop the sentence-completing work and immediately move to something more fitting). Thus, in truly directing, I am directed.

This means, among other things, listening not just to what is being said but also to what's *not* being said—and not only verbally but physically and emotionally. This listening—which is far from a passive activity!—allows us to deepen our resonance with clients so that we become an open and deeply attentive space for the optimal unfolding and expression of their process. In such listening, such dynamic receptivity, we can hear our intuition loud and clear, without any dilution of the attention we are giving our clients. Without clear and consistent access to our intuition, we will not be able to wisely use whatever methods we're employing and may tend to rely on them too much. In my way of working (and in my training/apprenticeship programs for psychotherapists and psychotherapists-to-be), intuition holds a far more central place than methodology.

Being directive is not the issue, since a good psychotherapist has to be directive, even when quietly listening to and mindfully holding the space for an extended monologue from a client. The issue is *how* we are being directive, how attuned we actually are to our clients' responses and what we are—or are not—doing. Are we being guided by our clients' needs and energies or are we being directed, however subtly, by our own need to be seen as a competent therapist? Are we being directed by our allegiance to a certain methodology? Are we being overly directive or not directive enough?

We are not just there with our clients' present situation but also with their past (which may in fact be very present), and we need to hold it all in our consciousness as we work, not just with regard to connecting the dots between past and present but also with regard to what moves our work in the most healing and effective possible directions.

The more we get out of our own way, and the more compassionately present we are, the more effectively we'll be able to serve our clients' real needs, regardless of how overtly directive we might need to be. If a client has a tendency to overadapt to what we're doing as a psychotherapist, we need to recognize this as soon as possible, skillfully expose it and its origins, and then work with it in a way that truly serves him or her.

Clients feel safest when they recognize that they are in the presence of a psychotherapist who is not only compassionate, grounded, and highly skilled but who can also help them to embody their own intrinsic authority even as they take charge with an authority that anchors and stabilizes the session.

There should be no doubt as to our leadership, however much we might allow, or might need to allow our clients to lead. They need to know—and not just intellectually!—that at any point we can take charge competently and compassionately and that we constitute a safe environment for their self-exploration and healing. So with artful skill, care, and reliability we guide the therapeutic flow even as we are guided by our clients' actions and needs.

Sometimes we might have the sense that we're simply a means through which the work happens, but even then we still need to be in charge of—and responsible for—our "mediumship." Our work is to wear our authority lightly but firmly, maintaining a solid yet fluidly alive presence with our clients, providing them a safe place to let go while neither relying upon nor necessarily imposing structure but letting it naturally arise from our relationship and interaction with them.

Being overly directive can do harm, but so too can *not* being directive enough. However gently or quietly we might wear the authority that comes with being in the position of psychotherapist, facilitator, guide, counselor, or teacher, that authority nonetheless is still there, and it's our job, our creative challenge, and sacred obligation, to embody it as caringly and proficiently as possible. The direction we bring to our sessions with our clients works best when it is guided by their real needs and by what they are doing with such needs.

As we learn not to rely upon or to necessarily impose structure but rather to let it naturally arise from our relationship with our clients, we wean ourselves from the security of operating from behind a set structure or methodology and instead open ourselves to an appropriately creative response. Such creativity keeps us fresh, open, and alert, as we engage in the art of intuitive integral psychotherapy.

Central to this art is the relationship between us and our clients, which takes shape through a blending of the following factors:

1. QUALITY OF THERAPIST PRESENCE. This has much to do with remaining fully present, both with regard to detail and to context; cultivating an attentiveness that is simultaneously detached and caring, panoramic and precise, relaxed and alert; developing and maintaining rapport; cultivating lucid empathy (with both enough distance to focus clearly and enough closeness to gather data that we could not otherwise access); being able to take charge with compassionate mastery; and being professional (this doesn't mean artificial distance but rather remembering and honoring the fact that the person before us is

there for a specific purpose and deserves the very best from us, regardless of our mood or state).
2. CLIENT PERMISSION FOR THERAPIST INTERVENTION. Such permission is normally present, at least to some degree, at the very beginning of psychotherapy. Its deepening and maintenance is necessary if the psychotherapy is to be effective, but it cannot and should not be forced. This does not mean passivity on our part; rather it means skillful navigation by us through the zone between trust and mistrust, which makes the therapeutic environment an ever-safer place.
3. WILLINGNESS OF THE CLIENT TO DO WHAT IS NEEDED. Clients commonly both want to work through whatever is obstructing their well-being and have resistance to doing so. Each impulse must be taken into account, and each must be treated with respect. Labeling resistance as wrong just creates

more resistance. When both we and our clients together can observe their resistance with compassion, their healing will accelerate. Client dependency upon us is not a problem when clients take charge—and are empowered to take charge—of their own work as much as they can. Then they will feel more that they are on the same team as us, as opposed to simply taking orders from us.

4. ALMOST COMPLETE FOCUS ON CLIENT. This does not mean losing touch with ourselves; giving our clients our undivided attention requires remaining attentive to ourselves and being fully present.

5. IN-DEPTH DIALOGUE. The conversation between us and our clients, however light or seemingly superficial, presents opportunity after opportunity for getting to the heart of the matter. Everything said can be an entry point into depth. Our clients' concerns will flavor, however subtly, whatever they say. They are skillfully invited to reveal what they would ordinarily conceal

and need to know that we are paying very close attention to what they are saying—and to what they are not saying—for their benefit. The psychotherapist-client conversation/encounter is at once a healing confessional, a portal into depth, a chance to become more conscious, an arena of mutual respect, and a chamber of discovery.

Intuitive integral psychotherapy—in which methodology is secondary to presence, care, and intuition—is a multidimensional art, working in depth with body, mind, emotion, spirituality, and social factors. As such, it is a fitting mix of doing and not-doing. If we are attached to our directing of our clients, we will very likely miss clues that are only obvious when we back off from having to run the show. In our not-doing—through which we are still wholeheartedly attentive to our clients—we are making space for them to more fully participate in their own healing. Then we and our clients are cocreating their needed healing and awakening in an atmosphere of mutual respect.

In intuitive integral psychotherapy's efficacious blending of sanctuary and crucible, powerful breakthroughs and realizations are inevitable, catalyzing psychospiritual healing and integration.

ILLUMINATING AND INTEGRATING BODY, MIND, EMOTION, AND SPIRITUALITY

In intuitive integral work, our mental, physical, emotional, social, and spiritual dimensions are encouraged to function and flow in organic tandem. Whatever issues or feelings arise are approached and engaged within the context of our innate wholeness of being in a manner that equally honors the personal, interpersonal, and transpersonal.

Without such connection, we are marooned from our natural integrity of being, over-identifying with particular aspects of ourselves at the expense of others. We may meditate deeply but find ourselves cut off from the depths of our emotions; or we may be able to access these depths but find ourselves getting overwhelmed by or too easily caught up in them; or we may change our way of thinking so that we can better regulate our emotions but find ourselves getting stuck in disembodied rationality. And we may conceal, unconsciously or not, aspects of ourselves that aren't very developed behind our strong suits.

The illumination and integration of our disparate elements—the fully embodied reunion of our scattered selves—is core work, providing us with the needed ground for transformation and further awakening. If we avoid such integration—as happens in spiritual bypassing—we deform rather than transform ourselves.

The following overview describes what it means to work in an intuitively integral context with our body, mind, emotions, and spirituality.

I. WORKING WITH OUR BODY

To work with our body is to be wholeheartedly attentive to it physically, energetically, psychologically, emotionally, and spiritually. To do this, we need to cease conceptualizing our body as a thing, a housing project, a mere container for our ego and supposedly higher dimensions. It is also useful to stop viewing our body as being "down there," somewhere below our head. When we view our body from our cranial headquarters, it may seem as if we are above it, and not necessarily just in a physical sense. We may even blame our body for bringing us down. But the fault lies not in our body, regardless of its condition, but rather in what we are *doing* with our body.

If the subtler messages of our body are not attended to, then more overt or dramatic signals of pain or distress may show up. If these are not given enough attention, even more blatant signs—like debilitating pain or dysfunction—may arise. Like the steed that needs only the hint of a command to respond, we must heed the language of our body when it is but a whisper and heed it with our full, undistracted attention.

When infused with mindfulness, body practices (hatha yoga, Rolfing, Feldenkrais, gym workouts, and so on) help us to more fully embody our fundamental nature. We begin to realize, more than just intellectually, that body and mind are not separate, that the body is the visible part of the mind and the mind the invisible part of the body. Then we are literally in touch with our innate wholeness of being. Such contact is the foundation, the ground, of healing. Hence the need to include the body in psychotherapy, whether through bringing more attention to it through appropriate questions or guided visualizations, or through actual hands-on contact in conjunction with psychotherapeutic direction.

By not letting the body speak its mind, we miss the wisdom that can arise from and through the awakening body; the body that is consciously lived, respected, and felt; the body that is full-bloodedly alive. So to bring about a deeper, more dynamic connection with our physicality, we need to work with our body both from the inside and out, in conjunction with psychoemotional work. This anchoring not only helps quiet and clarify our mind but also helps us to more fully embody our emotional and spiritual dimensions. The body asks only to be loved, lived, and illuminated. The body is not a burden with which we've been saddled. It is not an obstruction to wisdom or spiritual deepening!

We need to shift from having a body to being a body, and from being a body to Being. Then we can feel, in the flesh, how natural it is to be whole, no longer separating body and spirit. All we have to do is treat our body with respect and care, not holding its failings against it, becoming so intimate with our body that it ceases being an "it" and becomes reclaimed us, spirit-in-the-flesh.

II. WORKING WITH OUR MIND

How many of our thoughts do we actually think? Does not most of our mental activity arise seemingly unbidden, independent of a thought-generating thinker? And even when we seem to be clearly behind our thoughts—as when we are deliberately passing judgment on another—are we not then usually identified with such thoughts, entangled and all but lost in their weave?

Working with our mind means being consciously attentive to, and therefore not identified with, its various formations—thoughts, fantasies, comparisons, and judgments, all in constant flux. This awareness is not something of which our mind is capable; it is not a higher kind of thinking but rather a sentient openness. Only that which is beyond the mind can see or witness the mind.

As those who meditate know, thinking that we are aware is altogether different from *being* aware. To be aware of the actual process of thinking and to maintain that awareness for more than a few minutes is not easy. Our mind has a mind of its own, so to speak, and is not about to sit still or be quiet just because we want it to do so.

Nevertheless, we need to develop the ability to observe our mental activities with healthy detachment. Otherwise we are at the mercy of whatever winds happen to be blowing through our mind. As a certain thought arises, we automatically feed and solidify it with attention, letting ourselves be affected and guided by it while acting as if we are in charge. Becoming aware of what our mind is actually up to and realizing how difficult it is to maintain such a focus for very long is a humbling experience. The mind is a marvelous servant but a poor master. As we learn to relate to it rather than just from it, we find ourselves less entangled in our thoughts, regardless of our circumstances.

How can we do this? Discipline is needed—particularly in the form of sustained concentration—but so too is relaxation. Initially, we make the effort to stay focused on a particular object, like the sensations of our breathing, and once the chatter of our mind has significantly quieted down, our efforts lessen or perhaps even disappear, allowing us to settle into the uncluttered ease of innate awareness.

After sufficient practice, we'll find our capacities for concentration and relaxation mixing more and more naturally. This is the essence of meditative practice, not just in meditation but also in the midst of everyday life. In cultivating relaxed awareness, we come to inhabit the same relationship to our mental activities as does the sky to its clouds—not trying to get rid of them, neither suppressing nor indulging them. Awareness doesn't take sides; it shines equally on all that it touches.

If we are not present, we are not really living but are only dwelling in fantasies of past and future that won't give up the ghost. Awakening from such fantasies—and from all the entrapping dreams we regularly inhabit—is what meditative practice is all about.

Meditation is the art of allowing everything to be encompassed and penetrated by awareness. Meditation doesn't change the mind; it illuminates it. As we work with our mind, learning to witness its thoughts, beliefs, dreams, and interplay with our body and emotions, we are, in effect, cleaning house, immersing ourselves in the ever-fresh mystery of Being. This process often is best catalyzed not through meditative practices alone but through an artful combination with integrative psychological and body-centered approaches.

Even after plenty of meditative practice, we will very likely still find ourselves slipping into old habits of mind, but we don't have to consider this a problem. Getting derailed by our train of thought ought to be an occasion not for self-castigation but for healthy humility and humor. It's a chance to get back on track in a way that both lightens and strengthens us. Of course, we'll continue to have such lapses even after we're sure that we've learned the lesson by heart. The goal, however, is much deeper than perfection: it is to arrive as deeply as possible in the present moment, no matter what our state, letting all things serve our healing and awakening.

Compassionate attention gently stills our mind. When our mind is thus naturally quieted, the signals of our intuition and heart come through more clearly, allowing us to live more wisely.

Keep this in more than mind.

III. WORKING WITH OUR EMOTIONS

We're born feeling, we live feeling, and we die feeling. There is always some kind of feeling going on inside us, however much it might be in the background. Our emotions suffuse our flesh, mind, and psyche, layer upon layer. But how well do we know our emotions? How much at home are we with them? Do we have difficulty controlling or expressing certain emotions? We may know our IQ, but do we know our MQ (moral intelligence) and EQ (emotional intelligence)?

The shortage of emotional intelligence that plagues modern culture is largely rooted in the West's historical devaluing of emotion relative to cognition. We commonly view emotions as being "lower" or more "primitive" than reason, doing little more than clouding the skies of rational thought, muddying objectivity. Thinking clearly is thus often associated with dispassion, or a muting of our emotions. However, we can be strongly emotional and lucid at the same time, as when shedding tears makes us more articulate and insightful. Furthermore, the practice of dissociating ourselves from our emotions, especially our darker or more uncomfortable ones, can seriously disrupt our ability to think clearly and act morally. Neurological research demonstrates that impairments in emotional capacity, such as those caused by damage to brain regions essential for emotional processing, can actually retard our ability to make sound decisions.

Many factors need to be taken into account in examining a particular emotion, not the least of which is the interrelatedness of our emotions. Anger may be a defense against sadness, and sadness may be a defense against anger. Or anger and sadness may commingle, resulting in sullenness. Shame and fear may mix to produce guilt. And so on.

To work with our emotions is to become increasingly intimate with them. As obvious as it sounds, we need to know what we are feeling when we're feeling it. We learn the balance between containment (as when our anger is on the verge of mutating into aggression) and expression (as when held-in anger needs to be given an emphatically fiery voice). We need to learn how to regulate our emotions, how to directly express them, how to infuse their expression with awareness and compassion, how to ride, guide, and ultimately just be with them.

Let's take fear as an example. When we remain outside our fear, we remain trapped by it. So the key to working effectively with fear is to get inside it, which means, among other things, that we need to gain a clear knowledge of all the ways we have learned to get away from fear. Getting inside fear means getting under its skin, getting past its defining thoughts, past its propagandizing sentinels. Once we're within fear, our attention scanning our surroundings like a miner's headlamp, we can begin acquainting ourselves with its features, particularly those sensations and beliefs that together make it into a something we label "fear." The closer we get, the better we can see it. However, we also need to learn not to get close too quickly, not to move so fast that we can't keep digesting and integrating what we're experiencing.

When we consciously get inside our fear, we turn it inside out. Getting inside our fear with wakeful attention and compassion actually expands our fear beyond itself. Once the constriction at the center of fear ceases to be fueled, fear unravels and dissipates. In entering our fear, we end our fear of it.

Our emotions are not the problem! What matters is what we do with them. To cultivate intimacy with our emotions is to get close to them, really close, without getting lost or overly absorbed in them. Then we can accurately read and skillfully respond to whatever emotional weather we are experiencing, learning to ride our craft into the heart of the storm.

IV. WORKING WITH THE SPIRITUAL

Spirituality—the cultivation of intimacy with what we, in our heart of hearts, know to be sacred or ultimate—cannot be left out of any serious consideration of what it is to be human. As we become increasingly aware of our body, mind, and emotions, the question of identity almost invariably arises: *Who—or what—am I?* It is a question that seeks something more real than mind-made answers, a question that eventually brings us into a direct encounter with the ineffable reality of our existence.

Fully embodying our spirituality is a demanding but essential undertaking that must encompass our physical, mental, emotional, and social dimensions. Such spirituality is not removed from the stuff of everyday life but rather pervades and illuminates it with a perspective untainted by egoic or self-serving strategies.

Between the realm of pure Spirit, where all dualism vanishes, and the realm of ordinary egoic existence is the realm of Soul, which can be defined as individuated Being, or one's personalized essence. It is the last frontier of individuality. Soul is the face of spirituality. Beyond it lies undifferentiated Being. Soul has considerable transpersonal perspective, yet is still profoundly human; as much as it may stand in the transcendent, it usually remains intimate with the particular, the personal, the idiosyncratic, whether residing in saintly mansions or in the most appalling of slums. Soul keeps awareness from getting desiccated or overly detached.

To work with our soul is to open to it, to surrender to its perspective. This is an inherently vulnerable undertaking, in which we learn to make a truly major shift from avoiding our pain to directly moving toward and into it. Soul does not turn away from pain but instead meets it with compassion. With the openness that comes from integrating body, mind, emotion, and spirit, we discover the unity of Being that is our birthright. This is the fruit of wholehearted participation in healing and awakening practices. These practices include not only meditation and psychotherapy but every moment we are present. As we open spiritually, we realize that there is no such thing as an insignificant act. It all matters. And, because it all matters, nothing can be left out. This is why, sooner or later, we have to become intimate with *all* that we are. We cannot do this as ego-centered beings, but we can do it as soul-centered beings.

Spirituality is not an escape from life's difficulties; rather it is an embracing and illumination of them. When we recognize that each of us includes all traits and emotions—however much we might like to disown some of them—and when we can approach these with compassion, we cannot help but behave more compassionately (however fiercely!) toward others. Spirituality is love and awareness functioning as one.

Soul's embrace is both panoramic and particular, touching the universal without neglecting the personal and interpersonal. When its heart breaks, it breaks open and the circle of its reach is widened; its wounds only more deeply expose its love.

Ego says: I am what I think I am.

Soul says: I am more than I can imagine.

Spirit says: I am.

We are Light and we are Darkness

And we are the flesh, be it of mud or stars

Torn between the two

Yet already the One

Inseparable from the broken Many

ACKNOWLEDGMENTS

First of all, a deep bow to all of my teachers, not only for the transmission of their psychospiritual savvy but also for their slippages. Both were equally instructive.

A big thanks to Bill Kauth for suggesting I take my scattered writings on spiritual bypassing and turn them into a book, and to Jeff Brown for introducing me and my book-to-be to North Atlantic Books. Anne Connolly, my perspicacious editor, pushed me out of my literary comfort zone and pretensions of having a book that needed very little editing, inspiring me to make this a much more accessible book than it would have been otherwise. Thanks also to Laura Conley for her keen editorial suggestions.

Spiritual bypassing can be blatantly obvious and it can also be very subtle; my deep appreciation goes to all those who have had the courage to explore, illuminate, and uproot their own spiritual bypassing tendencies, including through psychotherapy.

A special thanks to those who have trained/apprenticed with me and my wife Diane, trusting us with their core wounds and longing to be truly free. Their willingness to go into their darkest places with our guidance continues to move me, fueling my deepening both in my psychospiritual work and in my writing.

And, most of all, my gratitude to Diane, my beloved and partner in all things, whose presence in my life serves me in more ways than I can imagine. Our uncommon bond and mutual embrace of what really matters is both familiar and ever-fresh, healing and awakening me. In the crucible and sanctuary that is our relationship, grace has me by more than the heart. And though we're together almost all of the time, never tiring of each other's company, I remain happily astonished every day that we are together.

ABOUT THE AUTHOR

Robert Augustus Masters, PhD, is the author of eleven books, including *Transformation Through Intimacy* and *Darkness Shining Wild*. He holds a doctorate in psychology and is a highly experienced psychotherapist, trainer of psychotherapists, and teacher of spiritual deepening. His integral, intuitive work dynamically blends the psychological and physical with the spiritual, emphasizing embodiment, authenticity, deep shadow work, emotional openness and literacy, and the development of relational maturity.

He has seen and personally experienced the highs and lows of spirituality (and spiritual bypassing) from many perspectives, including as a practicing psychotherapist for thirty-two years and as a spiritual teacher. Those who work with him are taught, among other things, how to turn toward and enter their pain so that they might pass through it rather than rise above or other- wise avoid it. At essence his work is about becoming more intimate with all that we are—dark and light, high and low, shallow and deep, neurotic and transcendent, dying and undying.

He and his wife Diane work and teach in very close conjunction, doing all their groups, sessions, and trainings together. To learn more about what they offer, visit www.robertmasters.com (where you can subscribe to his free newsletter, *The Crucible of Awakening*). They also offer online work; for more information go to www.masterscenterfortransformation.com.

Back Cover Material

"This timely and penetrating analysis of spirituality's shadow provides a much-needed counterpoint for those who tend to get blinded by its light."
—**STEPHEN BATCHELOR,** author of *Buddhism Without Beliefs*

Spiritual bypassing—the use of spiritual practices or beliefs to avoid dealing with painful feelings, unresolved wounds, and developmental needs—is so pervasive that it goes largely unnoticed in our culture. In the tradition of the landmark work *Cutting rough Spiritual Materialism by Chögyam Trungpa, Spiritual Bypassing* casts a lucidly critical eye on our deeply entrenched misuse of spirituality, furthering the body of psychological insight into how we use (and abuse) our spiritual practice in o. en unconscious ways.

While other authors have touched on the subject, this is the first book fully devoted to explaining and working through spiritual bypassing. Longtime psychotherapist Robert Augustus Masters provides an in-depth look at the unresolved or ignored psychological issues that are o. en masked as spirituality, including self-judgment, "confrontationphobic" compassion, excessive niceness, the demonizing of anger, and emotional dissociation. A must-read for anyone seeking increased self-awareness and a more integrated, compassionate relationship with themselves and others.

"There is much wisdom and good information in this book. Masters joins a growing number of wise teachers who understand that the personal and universal must be combined to bring true and genuine spiritual awakening."

—**JACK KKORNFIELD,** author of *A Path With Heart and A er the Ecstasy, the Laundry*

"Here is soul-fuel for those who would enter the road less traveled—the deeply examined life as part of spiritual practice."

—**JEAN HOUSTON, PHD,** author of *A Mythic Life*

"Clearly the most comprehensive and accessible treatment available on this crucial topic.... A great contribution to the ongoing integration of psychotherapy and spiritual practice, and to our understanding of the meaning of spiritual maturity."

—DONALD ROTHBERG, PHD, author of *The Engaged Spiritual Life Ecst*

ROBERT AUGSTUS MASTER,PHD is an integral psychotherapist, trainer of psychotherapists, and teacher of spiritual deepening (www.robertmasters.com).

Index

A

Abuse, *169, 171, 203*
Aggression, *126, 127, 152*
Anger,
  aggression vs., *126, 127, 152*
  approaches to working with, *127, 133*
  blind compassion and, *36*
  boundaries and, *152*
  compassion and, *133, 134*
  cultivating intimacy with, *122, 124, 136, 138, 139*
  heart-, *127, 133*
  identifying, *124, 126*
  -in, *127*
  judgment and, *136*
  mindfully held, *127*
  as 'negative' emotion, *25, 27, 32, 33, 119, 121*
  in others, *136, 138*
  -out, *127*
  repressing, *112, 113, 121*
  shame and, *222*
  violence and, *127*
Ascension and descension, *47, 48, 51, 52, 54*

B

Blame, *215, 216, 218, 224*
Body,
  distancing from, *191, 193, 194, 196, 198, 200, 210, 212*
  image, *196*
  integrating with, *193, 196, 198, 200, 202, 203, 205, 207, 210, 212, 213*
  memory of, *207, 208, 210*
Boundaries,

anger and, *152*
essentialness of, *141, 150, 152, 153*
freedom and, *141, 143*
healthy, *143, 145, 147, 150, 155*
intimacy and, *148, 155*
overdefined, *147, 150*
sex and, *171, 172*
spiritual bypassing and, *147, 148, 153, 155*
underdefined, *147, 148, 150*
Buddhism, *108, 110, 119, 152*
Busyness, *68*

C
Coincidence, *91, 101, 103*
  See also Magical thinking,
Compassion,
  anger and, *133, 134*
  blind, *35, 36, 38, 40, 42, 44, 45*
  essentialness of, *35*
  imitators of, *35*
  real, *44, 45*
Confrontation, avoiding, *40, 42*
Contraction vs. expansion, *28, 30*
Cultism, *233, 234*

D
Dalai Lama,
Descension and ascension, *47, 48, 51, 52, 54*
Detachment, *56, 86, 160, 162*
Dissociation, *47, 148, 180, 182*

E
Ego, *157, 158*
  See also Individuality,
Emotions,
  expressing, *32, 33*
  identifying, *124, 126*
  'negative', *25, 27, 28, 30, 32*

spiritual bypassing and, *9, 11, 12, 17, 18, 30*
Expansion vs. contraction, *28, 30*

F
Fear,
  blind compassion and, *36*
  as 'negative' emotion, *30, 32, 162*
  of pain, *87, 89*
  shame and, *263*
Forgiveness, *28*
Frankl, Victor, *5*
Freedom, *141, 143*
'Golden' shadow, *70*

G
Greed, spiritualized, *95*
Guilt, *216, 218, 224, 239, 265*

H
Hatred, *27, 28*
Heart-anger, *127, 133*
Humility, blind, *222*

I
Illness, responsibility for, *218, 220, 224, 225, 238, 239, 241, 242, 244*
Individuality, *157, 158, 160, 162, 163, 275*
Infancy, *183, 185*
Intimacy,
  with anger, *122, 124, 136, 138, 139*
  healthy boundaries and, *148, 155*
  lack of, in relationships, *61, 63, 155, 180, 187*

J
Judgment, *38, 40, 136*

K
Kornfield, Jack, *152*

L
Love vs. romance, *183*

M
Magical thinking,

appeal of, *97*
childhood origins of, *94, 95*
danger of, *97*
definition of, *91, 94*
egocentrism of, *101, 103*
healthy perspective on, *106*
as metaphor, *95*
prevalence of, *99, 101*
'signs' and, *99, 101, 103*
spiritual bypassing and, *91, 99*
'successes' in, *106*
synchronicity vs., *103, 105*
Maharshi, Ramana, *253*
Meditation, *89, 90, 302, 304, 305*

N
Nagarjuna, *254*
Negativity,
  characteristics of, *25, 27, 28, 30, 32, 33*
  spiritual bypassing and, *9, 11, 12, 17, 18*
  turning toward, *33*
Nonduality, *247, 248, 249, 251, 253, 254*
'No' saying, *36, 44, 152, 153, 171, 172*

O
Observer and observed, *97, 99*
Out-of-body experiences (OOBEs), *203*

P
Pain,
  avoidance of, *32, 83, 86, 87, 89*
  healing of, *90*
  meditation and, *89, 90*
  spiritual bypassing and, *9, 11, 17, 18, 20, 22, 23, 83, 86, 87, 89*
  storing, *207, 208*

turning toward, *83, 86, 87, 90, 202*
Personality, *157, 158, 160, 162, 163*
Pity, *35*
Positive thinking, *95, 238*
Projection, *188*
Prosperity consciousness, *95, 239*
Psychotherapy,
  devaluing of, *7, 18, 108, 110, 112*
  intuitive integral, *115, 287, 290, 292*
  shadow work and, *81*
  spirituality of, *112, 113, 115, 117*

R
Rationality, disembodied, *200*
Reality, self-creation of, *238, 239, 241*
Relationships,
  anger in, *136, 138*
  boundaries and, *155*
  confrontation in, *187, 188*
  lack of intimacy in, *61, 63, 155, 180, 187*
  romanticizing, *63, 180, 182, 183*
  spiritual bypassing and, *61, 63, 180, 182, 187*
  between spiritual teacher and student, *113, 115, 117*
Responsibility,
  blame vs., *215, 216, 218, 224*
  guilt and, *216, 218, 224, 239*
  for illness, *218, 220, 224, 225, 238, 239, 241, 242, 244*
  shame and, *222*
  spiritual bypassing and, *215, 220, 222*
Romance, *180, 182, 183, 185, 187*

S

S The Secret, *4, 239*
Self-help industry, *65*
Sex,
  boundaries and, *171, 172*
  conditioning and, *166, 171, 172*
  consent and, *166*
  cultural attitudes toward, *165, 166*
  maturity and, *174, 176, 177, 178*
  misuse of, *166, 176, 177*
  as release, *176*
  tantric, *169, 171, 174*
Sexual abuse, *169, 171*
Shadow work,
  definition of, *70*
  difficulty beginning, *77, 79*
  growing acceptability of, *72*
  psychotherapy and, *81*
  spiritual bypassing and, *72, 79*
  steps in, *73, 76*
  superficial vs. real, *72, 73, 79, 81*
  in supportive company, *76, 77*
Shame,
  anger and, *222*
  attitudes toward, *256*
  avoidance of, *256, 257, 263, 265*
  conversion of, *261, 263*
  guilt vs., *265*
  healthy vs. unhealthy, *257, 260*
  of others, *260, 261, 268*
  power of, *263, 265, 267, 268*
  spiritual bypassing and, *15, 257, 267*
  subtleness of, *268, 270*

working with, *267, 268, 270*
Spiritual bypassing, acknowledging, *15, 17*
aspects of, *4*
boundaries and, *147, 148, 153, 155*
as a business, *65, 227, 229*
cause of, *83, 86, 87, 89, 90*
cutting through, *15, 17, 18, 20, 22, 23*
darker emotions and, *9, 11, 12, 17, 18, 30, 119*
definition of, *2, 15*
fifth floor analogy for, *18, 20*
identifying, *273*
individuality and, *158*
magical thinking and, *91, 99*
nonduality and, *248, 249, 251, 253*
numbness and, *22, 23*
outgrowing, *11, 13, 23, 272, 273, 275, 277*
pain and, *9, 11, 17, 18, 20, 22, 23, 83, 86, 87, 89*
personal history and, *20*
pervasiveness of, *2, 4, 11, 23, 277*
psychological issues and, *7, 18*
relationships and, *61, 63, 180, 182, 187*
responsibility and, *215, 220, 222*
shadow work and, *72, 79*
shame and, *15, 257, 267*
signs of, *9, 17*
as spiritual shortcut, *60, 61, 63, 65, 68*
'successful', *18*
transcendence and, *47, 48, 51, 52, 54, 56, 58*
Spirituality, authentic, *5, 113, 272, 273, 275, 277*

conceptual, *22*
depersonalized, *158*
disembodied, *191, 193, 194, 196*
Eastern, *7*
gullibility and, *227, 229, 231, 233, 234, 235*
of psychotherapy, *112, 113, 115, 117*
'shortcuts' to, *60, 61, 63, 65, 68*
traps with, *12*
Spiritual teachers, psychotherapy and, *108, 110, 112, 113, 115, 117*
students' relationship with, *113, 115, 117*
Superstition, *94, 99, 101*
See also Magical thinking,
Synchronicity, *103, 105*

T
Tantric sex, *169, 171, 174*
Thich Nhat Hanh, *112*
Thoughts, power of, *97*
Tolerance, blind, *222*
Transcendence,
definition of, *47, 56*
healthy, *47, 54, 56, 58*
spiritual bypassing and, *47, 48, 51, 52, 54, 56, 58*
unhealthy, *47, 58*
Trauma, *207, 208*

V
Violence, *127*

W
Welwood, John, *2*
'Yes' saying, *36, 150, 152, 166*

www.ingramcontent.com/pod-product-compliance
Lightning Source LLC
Chambersburg PA
CBHW060552230426
43670CB00011B/1794